The Secret to Marriage

A Step by Step Guide to Creating a Loving and Lasting Marriage

The Secret to Marriage

A Step by Step Guide to Creating a Loving and Lasting Marriage

Copyright © 2016, Eric Rios

All rights reserved. No part of this publication may be reproduced, stored in a retrieval system, or transmitted by any means—electronic, mechanical, photographic (photocopying), recording, or otherwise—without prior permission in writing from the author.

Although the author and publisher have made every attempt to ensure the accuracy and completeness of the information contained in this book, we assume no responsibilities for errors, inaccuracies, omissions, or any other inconsistency herein.

Managing editor: Kristen James – www.writerkristenjames.com

Cover Design by, Vinesh Kumar J V - www.akivda.com – A Creative Digital Design Agency

Published in the United States by The Smiling Marriage, LLC

ISBN: 978-0-692-61348-1

Table of Contents

Foreword 6

Dedication 7

A Note from the Author 8

Introduction 10

Chapter 1: Answers to some really important questions 14

    How Long Will It Take? 14

    Why did this Happen? 16

    Can I Change my Spouse? 18

    Can This Marriage System Really Work? 25

Chapter 2: Understanding divorce and its consequences 32

    The Real Cost of Divorce 33

    Should you Work on Your Marriage or Get Divorced? ... 39

Chapter 3: Letting go of what's not working 50

    #1 - Set Aside Your Problems 52

    #2 - Look at Your Relationship from a Different Perspective 55

    #3 - Open Yourself Up To Change 57

    #4 - Let Go of Past Issues 63

#5 – Let Patience Become your Best Friend 68

Chapter 4: Planning a new strategy 76

Step #1: Recognize that you can't force change on your spouse. 77

Step #2: Changing yourself first is the most important part of change when it comes to your relationship. 80

Step #3: "What if I change and my spouse doesn't?" 84

Step #4: How long should it take before I see some change? 86

Step #5: Change will start with a new focus 89

Chapter 5: Building a new marital value system 94

The 90/10 Rule 95

Creating a Marriage Plan 99

Who You Want to Be 101

What Kind of Marriage Do You Want? 105

Creating Lasting Habits 108

Chapter 6: Working the plan for a great marriage 114

#1 - Make Your Relationship Come First 115

#2 - Developing the Habit of Love 119

#3 - Working the Habit of Love – Taking Ownership 123

#4 - Sitting Next to the Fireplace 126

#5 - Making Love Last 129

Chapter 7: Affair proofing your marriage 134

    Keeping Trust Alive in your Marriage (or rebuilding trust) 135

    Signs to Look For 141

    Preventing Your Own Affair 145

    Preventing Your Spouse's Affair 149

    Keeping Your Relationship Alive 152

Chapter 8: Kids & Step Kids 158

    Mean What You Say 161

    Parental Involvement 163

    "His" Kids 169

    "Her" Kids 171

    Step Kids 173

Chapter 9: 52 Weeks of Love 182

Foreword

Have you ever told a secret? Have you ever wanted to know the secret that everyone is talking about? Secrets can be exciting and fun. Everyone loves secrets and the author, Eric Rios, will be sharing a very important secret with you that you will not want to miss. This is the secret that every married couple or soon to be married couple is looking for. It's <u>The Secret to Marriage</u>!! Eric has studied marriages and relationships for years and with his own experiences he will share with how to make a marriage last; how to have the best marriage; and how to improve your marriage. Have you ever looked at couples celebrating their 25th, 50th or 75th wedding anniversaries and wonder how they did it? Me too and having been married to the author for almost 10 years I am understanding now how to make a lasting marriage. Just like in life, practice makes perfect for marriages too. You will learn from this book how to help make your marriage last. You took the wedding vow (or soon will be) on that one day but it's all the days of your marriage that you should vow to make this the best marriage you possibly can. I love how my husband wants to help so many people with their relationships. He has a heart for this and I hope you enjoy this book as much as I do.

- Shelly Rios

Dedication

This book is dedicated to all the married couples out there in the world. Whether this is your first marriage, your second marriage, third marriage or whichever it may be. I know one thing, no matter which marriage you are on, you deserve the very best marriage ever. You deserve to wake up every day still in love with your spouse and always excited to see them. You deserve to have a Smiling Marriage, one that you are very proud of.

Please use this book as a guide to stay conscious about keeping love alive in your marriage and home.

"The greatest gift we have all been given each day is the gift of choice." ~ Eric Rios

Go make your marriage great!!!

A Note from the Author

We as a human race seem to always want to find the simplest solutions to almost any problem we face. We are looking for the easiest way out. We look for the secrets on how to make money, lose weight, read faster, learn quicker, have a better relationship, and the list can go on and on. While writing this book I knew it was important to include the secret to having a good marriage.

Many of you who read this book will read with hopes of finding the secret as quickly as possible and many of you will just read the book learning different things you can use on a daily basis to make your marriage better. Please let me tell you that as you read this book I will reveal the Secret to Marriage many times. It is revealed in every chapter of this book. Each one of you may find that it is something different but I can assure you that the Secret to Marriage is very simple and it is one thing.

I hope you enjoy taking the time to read this book and I know that once the Secret has been revealed to you and you start acting on what the Secret is, your marriage will start seeing the fruits of your new choices. The Secret to Marriage awaits you as you read.
Eric F. Rios

Introduction

After having my own failed marriages I realized that there had to be a better way. I knew that there had to be something that I could do to have a better marriage. I would see married couples all over the place that appeared to be happy. Surely I could do the same thing they were doing and have my own great marriage. Surely having a great marriage wasn't just a myth.

I found myself starting all over again. For many of us this can be quite a struggle to have to start life all over again. We all want to be loved and cared for by someone. This is a very scary time, we are now vulnerable like never before. Our lives have been shattered and turned upside down. Our trust has been violated by our partners. We are hurt and in pain.

For those of us who have kids, we now find ourselves feeling like we are alone in raising our kids. We look at our kids and see the hurt and pain that they are suffering. We see them cry and take the blame for the marriage falling apart. Many times they are told it was their fault. The pain of the broken marriage doesn't just affect us, but it affects all of those around us.

The brokenness that we feel when we walk into that court room is devastating. We are now having a judge and a bunch of attorneys dictate what our new life is going to look like. Our finances are destroyed. For many they find themselves having to get a job for the first time in many years. We lived as the home maker as our spouse was the financial provider for the home. There has to be a better way I tell myself.

Now we find ourselves looking again for a new partner. This is the daunting challenge that we hoped we would never have to face again. We think to ourselves maybe this one will work out. Our kids are now exposed to someone who they will be expected to respect and love. Our kids are the ones now who find themselves in this place of anger and hurt as they now have to deal with the new parents who may not even like them at all. They take this pain and hide it deep down inside of themselves. They show it in school by their behaviors, their grades and in many cases by hurting themselves.

There has to be a better way I tell myself. No matter who I fall in love with and no matter where I go I am still there. I have not changed anything about myself and find myself back in the same position when I get married again. I feel alone again and unhappy and unfulfilled. My kids are angry with me, my family is disappointed in me. My life feels like it is such a mess. I have shed too many tears and I find myself dying inside. I want so badly to just Smile again. I want so badly to not to feel the pain of disappointment again. All I want, is to wake up with someone who loves me and cherishes who I am as man or woman.

Someone who will make me feel safe, make me feel loved and cared for. All I want is for my kids to not have to feel the pain of disappointment anymore. I want to see my kids smile again inside.

Our pain is real, our suffering is real, our broken heart is real, but I want to share that there is a better way. I found a better way, being married doesn't have to be so hard, and our kids don't have to suffer the pain of our choices. I have found a better way.

Over 11 years ago I realized that in order for my marriage to ever have a chance I had to make some changes in my own life first. I realized that every action I take has a result linked to it. I know now that with the simple system I use in being married, I find myself waking up every day happy and excited to be married to the person I am married to.

You ask, what did you do differently? I ask that you read the book and use it as your guide to create your own great marriage. There is no fix all for anything in this life. But I promise you that your marriage can be better and it can Smile again.

Chapter 1

Answers to some really important questions

Are you excited about where you are and where you're going in your marriage and your life? No? Well, you're in the right place. This book is going to help you change your life for the better. Your marriage is going to be so much better. First, there are some answers I need to discuss to some really important questions.

How Long Will It Take?

The number 1 question I hear is, "How long is it going to take for my marriage to get better?"

Some variations include, "How long is it going to take for me to get results? How long is it going to take? Is it going to happen overnight?" You're probably wondering when you'll see results. It won't be overnight. Not going to happen.

"Is it going to happen in a week?" It possibly could.

"Is it going to happen in a month?" It possibly could, but understand something: When it comes to fixing human beings, individuals, and couples, time is your friend. Understand, it's going to take a little bit of patience on your part with you doing the right things at the right times. That's what will create great results for you. Don't be in a hurry. Don't think that you've got to make it all happen overnight. Don't be in such a hurry that you think, "Man, why isn't that happening?" If you go that route, you'll get frustrated and want to give up. Please remember to go a little slower to get the results you really want, because you don't want to create an instant result that will go away.

You've heard the stories of people winning the lottery. They won this huge sum of money just like that, but then all of a sudden they're filing for bankruptcy two years later. This is going to be something like that. You don't want to jump into "all of a sudden it's better" when you haven't really changed who you were. Instead, you just found something to make it better quickly. Things that happen quickly generally go away quickly as well. I want you to take the time to develop yourself as an individual in your relationship, using the tools in this book to help you and your spouse become better parents, better husbands, better wives, and better people in general. Let's get started!

Why did this Happen?

Another big question I often hear is, "Why did God let my marriage turn into such a mess?" First of all, I don't think God let your marriage turn into a mess. I think we as human beings let our marriages turn into a mess. If you have kids, you'll understand this well. You can tell your kids 100 times to do something a certain way, and they're still going to do it their way. They may never, ever, ever take ownership of what they're doing until they realize what they did was wrong. They have to see the negative impact it had on them. Imagine if your kid looked at you and said, "Well, why did you let me turn my life into such a mess?" You're going to look at your kid and you're going to say, "Well, let me tell you something. I laid out a roadmap for you. I showed you what you should do. I showed you how you should do it. I gave you all these tools to make your life ultimately better, but you still wanted to make your own choices."

It wasn't God who caused or allowed your marriage to turn into a mess. It was we as human beings, and a lot of that comes from how we were raised, our preconditioned responses, and our conditioned responses to things that happened, and our habitual behaviors that we've developed over time. All these things play a huge part in why our marriage has turned into a mess, but that's okay. The cool thing about anything is, it can change. You can change your marriages direction in a moment's notice. It can absolutely get better! I'm sure if you have kids, you've seen it happen where they finally get it. Then, you're so excited. You're like, "I've been telling you this for years." Then, they're like, "Yeah, Mom, I know, I should have listened to you. Yeah, Dad, you were right. Maybe you were a little smarter than I thought you were."

This is just human nature. We want to do things our way without really looking for the best way. We just want to do it the quickest way possible and never really look for what's worked in someone else's life, how has it benefited them, and what they did that we could try.

We're going to learn some really cool things, so let's get excited about this. Let's not sit there looking at our marriages as if it's the end of the world. No, let's look at our marriage as, "There's a new hope. There's a new hope in town. There's a new sheriff in town." You're the sheriff, and the sheriff gets to make changes. Isn't that cool that the sheriff is going to make the new changes, and you are the sheriff. Do you know where the changes are going to start? They're going to start with you.

Can I Change my Spouse?

Your marriage is not going to change with you trying to change your spouse. I'm telling you, you can't change your spouse. Your spouse will have to change themselves. You're never going to change your spouse, but due to your actions and behaviors, your spouse is going to want to make changes for you. Your spouse is going to want to make changes that you're going to fall in love with, because at one point in your relationship, you loved that spouse, otherwise you wouldn't have married him or her. You fell in love with that individual. There are going to be some things you need to do. This is the work part that's going to help you change your spouse through your behaviors, not through anything you tell them to do.

Psychologically, when you tell someone what to do, you automatically bring up a defense mechanism. They don't want to do it. If you ask somebody to do something, they're more inclined to do it. In marriage, when there's been all this bickering, all this fighting, and all these arguments for so long, even if you ask, it still doesn't do any good at all. It just doesn't make any difference, because they're already bitter and they're already angry. You can't just change your spouse. They can't just change you, either. You have to change *you* first, and make you the best husband or the best wife that you could possibly ever be. While you do this, you're going to see changes in your spouse because they're going to see changes in you. They're going to wonder, "Why is she treating me so nice?" and "Why is he buying me flowers?"

When a husband comes home and brings his wife flowers, the first thing the wife thinks is, "All right, what do you want?" I think this all the time with my kids especially. My daughter will come in and say, "Dad, I love you. I love you Dad." I'm like, "Okay, Faith, what do you want?" I get that, and with spouses, this happens all the time. We think because they do something nice that there's an ulterior motive. I'm going to teach you how to do those nice things without an ulterior motive. You may not want anything at all, but at the end of the day, you want a great marriage, and you deserve a great marriage. Becoming a better you is the most important thing you could ever do for your marriage.

Let me share something. If you get divorced, remember one thing: you take you with you. No matter where you go, you always go with you. We know that 50% of all first marriages end in divorce. 60% of all second marriages end in divorce. 75% of all third marriages end in divorce. The odds are against you if you keep leaving one marriage to go to the next. Maybe we should stop, take a look, and say, "Well, maybe I'm the problem. Maybe it wasn't my spouse. Maybe I'm a part of the problem."

The whole point of this book is to get you to see how you can create the most amazing marriage ever. You're going to fall in love with your spouse all over again. They're going to fall in love with you all over again. Your life is going to change in ways you never dreamed.

When you were boyfriend and girlfriend, in most cases it was an amazing relationship. You were in love. Your marriage can be exactly the same. Your marriage can absolutely be exactly what you want it to be when you and your partner make it a priority.

Question Number 3 is, "Why do some marriages fail and others thrive?" Have you ever looked at your friends and wondered, "Why do they have such a good marriage and why do we have such a bad marriage?" Have you ever seen maybe your parents, your grandparents and seen that they were married for 10 years, 20 years, 30 years, 50 years, 60 years, and just asked, "What did they do differently? What did they change? How are they different? What things did they do that I'm not doing? What made that marriage such a great marriage? Why is mine so hard?" It's not that your marriage is so hard. It's just our choices that we make on a daily basis, our priorities, and our intentions that are causing us so much pain in the relationship.

Our lack of priority in our marriage is causing us pain. Our lack of intention in our marriage is causing us pain. Our lack of attention to our spouse is causing us pain. There're so many things we're doing that's causing us pain, and we don't even realize it. These are the behaviors that you do every single day. We're conditioned by our daily behaviors. Your response to your spouse if he or she says something is a conditioned behavior. We have to recondition and retrain who we are and what we want in order for us to have a great marriage. You can't just hope to God that your marriage is going to be great. You can't live on a hope and a dream that it's going to get better. You have to intentionally go out of your way to make your marriage better. You have to raise your standards and look at yourself and say, "Hey, I am responsible for creating a great marriage."

Did you hear the word "create"? You need a blueprint. If you build a house, you're going to start with a blueprint. To make that blueprint, you're going to look at an end product. You're going to look at exactly what you want first, and then you're going to build the blueprint around that. Then, you're going to take step by step processes in order to achieve the result, and that's a beautiful home that you decided to build. Our marriage is the same way. We need to create a great relationship. It's just not going to happen all by itself. No matter what you do, you can't just expect your marriage to be great like your friends' or somebody else's. You have to decide what it is you want out of your marriage, and what you're willing to give up to get what you want in your marriage.

Remember, if you leave this marriage, you take you with you. You may think you are perfect, but more times than not from what I've seen, those spouses who leave end up divorced again or end up in a pitiful, miserable, down in the dumps relationship. Their lives are just in such turmoil. I want you to get this today. I'm so passionate about this because you deserve a great marriage. You deserve a marriage that inspires you to live and to wake up every single day excited about the life long decision you have made. I've seen so many men who come to work and they don't want to go home to their spouse. There are women who will go to work, and at the end of the day, they don't want to go home. All they see is how ugly their marriage is. They see no hope. They feel no hope. They feel desperate inside for something to be better. They're yearning for just a little bit of love and a little bit of attention.

They share these problems with those at work and discover others share the same problems. Then, you begin to see less hope, and less hope, and less hope. But I'm going to tell you this. Your marriage can work, and your marriage can be great. Your marriage can be the best marriage you've ever imagined. Your marriage can be absolutely 100% a marriage that you just fall absolutely in love with. Think about this, "Will my marriage make it and stand the test of time?" It absolutely can. Every marriage can make it and every marriage can stand the test of time. You just have to decide and see that this is important to you and that you want to make it work and you're willing to make it work. If you're not willing to do the work, no matter what I say, no matter what any counselor says, no matter what any coach says, you're wasting your time.

The best part is, Marriage is pretty simple when you both know what you want, and you both can work towards a common goal and have common interests. It's not that one may like football, one may like soccer, one may like ballet, one may like dance. You have a man who wants to watch TV and a woman who wants to decorate the house and make it look really pretty. A woman wants to do yard work. The man doesn't want to do any yard work. It's about you and your spouse having a plan and a goal to work towards.

You're going to learn all those things in this book. You're going to learn how to make your marriage great. Making your marriage great is really simple. It's simple for both you and your spouse. I don't care where your relationship is right now, it can and will be better if you'll just apply these principles. Remember, there's no guarantee to anything. I can't guarantee that your marriage is going to last, but I can guarantee that your marriage can ultimately be better if you'll just apply some simple principles to your life that will create a better life, a better marriage.

Can This Marriage System Really Work?

The final question for this chapter is, "Will this marriage system really work?" Many people get a book but never read through Chapter One. I've even heard it said as much as 60% of people never read another nonfiction book after they graduate high school or even graduate college. I'm not going to make these chapters long. I'm just going to put into each chapter what I think needs to go into it, so you'll take the time to read it, to embrace it, and to define the solution to the problems that you're having. We go back to the question, "Will this work?" Anything can work, if you'll work the system. Anything can work, if you'll do the things necessary to make your marriage great.

I was listening to John Maxwell a very well-known author and speaker, he was sharing that he got into marriage counseling many years ago. He said, "But this wasn't for me. I couldn't do this. This drove me nuts. I would have these couples come to see me, and the couple would come in and share all of their problems, and I'd tell them what they needed to do. Then, a week later they'd come back with the exact same problems. I would ask them, 'Did you do what I told you?' They'd look at me and say, 'Well, no I didn't really do what you said because I just, uh, well, I just didn't really think it was going to work, so I really just didn't do it.' I would become so frustrated, and think, how am I supposed to help them if they're not willing to help themselves?"

I know another counselor, and she always tells her clients that, "If I'm going to work harder on your marriage than you are, then we shouldn't even waste our time." You've got to put the time in. You've got to put the work in. Remember this, the work isn't that hard. These are just simple procedures and techniques to help you change how you think about your marriage, how you see your marriage, and how you see your mindset. Your whole idea and perception of marriage is going to change because you're going to understand marriage. You're going to understand why you were so much in love as boyfriend and girlfriend. You're going to understand why you aren't so much in love now as husband and wife. These things are not hard.

To the men, make this a priority. As a man, I look at us as the leaders of the home. This isn't being sexist, but this is just it. I look at myself as a leader in my home. I am the one who leads by example. If I want my wife to be someone who loves, to be caring, to be kind, I need to be loving and caring and kind. Men, I would never tear down the man as I see this happen so many times in relationship counseling. I'm not here to do that at all. I support the man. I'm going to help you men to lift yourself up above and to raise your standards. This way, you will be the one leading by example.

Women, ladies, it's up to you just as well to lead by example. We want things to happen in our relationship, but we need to give attention to those things that we want. It works both ways.

Guys, ladies, husbands, wives, let's make this work. Let's make this an amazing relationship because as we go into Chapter 2, we're going get into the meat of things. We're going to start helping you change how you see your marriage. Your marriage is going to change in such a way that you're going to ask yourself, "Why didn't I have this sooner? Why didn't I have all this information when I first got married? I could have created such an amazing marriage and saved myself some gray hair, some losing my hair, stressful days, some teary eyes, some broken homes, and some brokenness."

I understand divorce very well. I've been there. I've been married and divorced. I understand that very well. I understand the good, the bad, and the ugly. I understand 100% that so much of my marriage was my fault, from me just not knowing. You don't know what you don't know sometimes, but I take responsibility for the things that I did and I did not do. I understand where you could possibly be in a child support issue, in a case where your husband or your wife is threatening to take the kids because the relationship is breaking apart. I understand where you're coming from. I understand what it's like to have to go to court and have your kids ripped out from under you. I understand what it is to get custody of your kids. I understand all the things that come along with the divorce. I understand how the financial aspect can just destroy your life. I understand how it can cause you to go into bankruptcy.

I understand how it can cause every part of your life to feel like you have no more control, but I'm telling you, I was blessed to find a great system. Thirteen years ago, I looked at my marriage and said to myself, "Why is my marriage so bad? Why is it falling apart?" I began to develop a system that allowed me to create a new Me, a new mindset about women, a new mindset about marriage. I've applied this system for the last 11 years, and I'm happily married. I love my wife. I love my marriage. I love what we have. The system is so easy to follow. I have to tell you, this is the easiest thing you'll ever get to do, but it requires you to take the time, make some priorities, and change some priorities in your life to make this system work for you. Are you ready to get started and change your life?

"Men marry women with the hope they will never change. Women marry men with the hope they will change. Invariably they are both disappointed."
— *Albert Einstein*

If you find yourself in need of 1 on 1 marriage coaching, couples marriage coaching, or an intensive workshop, (Marriage by Design Workshop), contact us via website: **www.thesmilingmarriage.com**.

Chapter 2

Understanding divorce and its consequences

I have a surprising truth to share with you. It's not a secret, but it's something we don't think about often. ***The one thing that we've been given every single day of our life, is the gift of a choice.*** That's right; we've been given the gift of a choice. God looked down upon each one of us and said, "Look, today I give you the gift of choice. Today you can look at your marriage and say, 'It'll never work,' or you can look at your marriage with a new perspective and say, 'I've got a choice to make it work.'"

Choices have consequences, and divorce is no different. It's important to understand the consequences of divorce. First, just consider the cost of a divorce: it's going to cost you a lot of money, a lot of heartache, and a lot of tears. The average divorce in the United States costs $53,000 if you own a home. $53,000. If you own a home you're going to have to buy the other person out of the house. Refinance the house. Maybe sell the house and both of you have to move into different places. Your kids have to change schools. Think of all the turmoil you're going to have. Now you have the attorney fees. Now you have child support, now you have alimony. That's a lot of things you're going to have in this divorce. Think of others before you decide to get divorced. We're talking about this because I want to make sure you understand the consequences of your divorce.

The Real Cost of Divorce

That's not even the real cost of divorce. I had a discussion with a diverse group of thirteen year old female teenagers a while back. Some were from broken homes and some weren't. This was at my house at my kitchen table with some of my daughter's friends. They were all sitting around a table chatting. I like to talk to people. I don't care if you're a teenager or you're an old person or what you are, even if you're a dog I might just talk to you. I looked over there at this group of girls, and I said, "Let me ask you a question. What are your thoughts on marriage?"

Can you imagine what some of the responses were? They were all so honest with their response. Not one of them held back. This is about the consequences of divorce. I want you guys to get the big picture here of understanding what's going to happen when you get divorced. If you make divorce your choice, one of your options, you need to understand that if you have kids it's going to really affect them in some way. Some kids get through it easier; some kids get through it harder. Some kids are punished through it. Some kids feel guilty. There are so many issues that kids are going to have if you decide to get divorced.

That's why I wanted to share this short interview with a group of thirteen year old girls. It's eye opening. Of course, I won't share any names because that really doesn't matter. What matters is that you understand what was said. When I asked the question, "What do you think about marriage?" the very first response out of one of the kid's mouth was, "It doesn't last." Did you hear that? The very first response out of one of the kid's mouth was, "It doesn't last."

That's sad that you have a thirteen year old teenager whose perspective and idea of marriage is that it doesn't last, it doesn't work out, it's never going to work. The greatest part about teenagers is they just open up and spill everything out with no filter at all. This teenager began to tell me, "Now my parent has a girlfriend and they fight all the time. All they ever do is fight. They bicker, they argue, they fight, they fight, they fight, they fight, all they do is just argue. They never get along at all."

When I heard her say this I was thinking to myself, "Wow, so you jumped out of the pot into the frying pan." Maybe if we look at it from a different perspective, we think well, maybe we're the problem. Maybe we need to change something internally to get a different external result, which is a better relationship.

One of the other girls said, "Well, I think marriage is good. Marriage isn't bad at all." Her parents had been together for a long time. She said, "My parents get along very well. They have a lot of fun. They do things together. They do things with the kids." A good balanced life.

Then another teenager said, "Well, there's just a lot of fighting and there's divorce. It's just ugly. It just doesn't work out. So many people get divorced, they're unhappy."

I hope you get where I'm going with this. Hearing these thirteen year old kids tell me their thoughts on marriage was eye opening. Most parents don't realize how their divorce will affect their children.

Now we have some of these kids who are in a stepparent family, which can be an enormous challenge for the kids. And remember, the kid never asked to be put into that situation. That child never asked to be put into that home. That child never asked to see that divorce happen. That child never asked to be brought into your drama, into your own misery, but the child was born into your home. We bring the children into this world and this is the perspective they end up having.

We could ask thousands of kids and we would get different answers from every kid. Some kids blame themselves. Some kids blame their parents. Some kids hate their parents. I know so many different couples where the children hate the stepparent, or the children don't respect their parent because of the circumstances and the situations. There was an affair. They look at the person who had the affair as the worst person in the world. *How could you do this to my mom? How could you do this to my dad? Were they not good enough for you?* That's how teenagers see things so many times. We put them into this situation.

When you consider a divorce, consider the ramifications you're going to have on yourself and your kids. Think about what the kids will feel, and how they're going to act and react. Remember, if you decide to get remarried, you're taking you with you. You're taking all of your issues with you into the new relationship. On top of that, you're expecting your child or children to jump into this new relationship with you and to accept all the junk that comes along with it. Be careful. Be thoughtful. Be mindful of the decision you're about to make when it comes to your marriage. Your kids deserve a great marriage just as well as you do. That great marriage is something they share in.

I watched a show the other day about a parent and a stepparent who told their child who was sixteen years old, "If you weren't in our life, our relationship would be so much better." My first thought was wow, how do we tell these kids who had no control over the situation, that if they were gone our lives would be ultimately better? How do we do that? Why do we do that? I felt so bad for this child. No wonder this child is reaching out to drugs and to alcohol and to doing things they shouldn't. They don't feel welcome and wanted at home.

I'm trying to tell you this because I want you to consider your options before you consider divorce. The divorce is going to affect your children in such an adverse way.

Is it possible for kids to come through a divorce all right? Yes, some kids can also come through a divorce and do very well. Both my wife and I have children from other marriages that have come through a divorce. They are much loved, they are cared for, and they're treated well. They're respected, and their feelings are respected and honored. We make sure our kids are an absolute priority when it comes to the relationship. We live a life in front of our kids that we would love to see them live.

This is the responsibility you have to take on when you decide to get divorced. You've got to become a constant in your kid's life. You can't bash the other parent. You can't go calling them names or talking bad about them. You just don't do those things in front of your kids because, first of all, your kids don't deserve that. What your kids deserve is to see you be the example you would want them to live.

I just want you to realize how important your kids are and see the consequences if you decide to get divorced. Your kids are going to go through this custody battle, where this parent is saying, "Hey, I want the kids. I'm taking the kids away from you." This kid is going to feel pulled both ways by each parent. We're tearing our kids apart sometimes with our choices of divorce. But hear this; there's no judgment here at all on any person because I have been divorced. I understand where you are. I understand what it is like to be on both sides of the custody battle. I'm just trying to get you to understand how important it is to take your kid's thoughts and emotions, and just keep them in mind. Realize that they are children and they need love. They need to see you love and to be loved.

Should you Work on Your Marriage or Get Divorced?

You can turn any marriage around. Your marriage can be great, and your kids need to see that it can be great. I want you to ask this question: should I get divorced? I don't condone divorce at all. I don't think divorce is the best solution to anything. I think the best solution is figuring out how to make your marriage work. Well, you ask, "Then why did you get divorced?" Sometimes it just happens and there's no control over it. There's nothing you can do about it. I didn't want to get divorced. Nobody gets married with the desire to get divorced. That's not how marriage is supposed to work.

Vows say, "Till death do us part," but so many people go into the marriage with, "Well, if it doesn't work out, we'll just get divorced." As long as you leave that as an option, you're probably going to use it. I want to eliminate that option in your life. I don't want you to see divorce as your option. I want you to see working your marriage out and creating an amazing marriage as your only option.

You say, "It's not possible, there's no way we can do this. We've been married for ten years and I hate him," and, "I hate her." You say, "We don't get along. All we do is fight." Do you ever wonder why? Do you ever take the time to think about why you fight? I'll go into that more later as I share how to change all those things.

We're looking at the question, "Should I get divorced?" I'm going to tell you no. I want you to make your marriage a priority and make it work. I want you to make your marriage a priority just like you would your job. Make your marriage a priority as if it is the only thing on earth you have. You deserve to have a good marriage. You deserve to wake up in the morning next to the person you love. You deserve to go to bed every night next to the person you love. When I go to bed at night, I cannot wait to lie next to my wife. When I get up in the morning, I look forward to lying next to my wife. This is where your relationship needs to be.

You're not looking for a perfect relationship. What you're looking for is a relationship where you're both happy. You're both excited. You both want to see each other. You've learned to create love in your relationship. We go back to: should I get divorced? No. Don't get divorced. Give it your all first. Look at life with a new perspective and a new set of eyes. Look at life in such a way that you say to yourself, "Well, maybe I should just give it one more chance. Maybe if we try something different."

The definition of insanity is what? Doing the same thing over and over and over and over again, expecting different results. Most of the time in relationships, that's what it is. We try the same thing over and over. We focus on the same things over and over, and we wonder why in the world is it not getting any better? Why in the world is it so bad?

The last question I have here is this: is there really hope for my marriage? Holy cow, Batman, there's definitely hope for your marriage, there's hope for any marriage. "What if I want my marriage to work and my spouse doesn't want my marriage to work? Is there still hope for my marriage?" There's always hope for your marriage. There's always hope just as long as you have breath, and as long as they have breath. Your marriage can absolutely work. You ask, "Well, what I do then?" We're going to start here, where your spouse doesn't want to make it work and you do.

Let's start with this; patience is going to become your best friend. Understand that you're not going to make this perfect overnight, so patience is going to become your best friend. If your spouse wants to make it work, patience is going to still become your best friend. You guys are going to both have to work at things together with a different mindset. We're going to look at different ways to create the marriage you want to have. Remember in Chapter 1, we talked about having a blueprint. We talked about having a common goal for our marriage. We talked about creating a marriage based on an end result that we wanted. That end result is going to be, "Well, I want a great marriage."

So what is a good marriage? What is a great marriage? What does that look like to you? Not to me, because I may see a great marriage as something completely different. When we look at that hope for your marriage, I want you to realize that you can start right now, right this very moment, creating the marriage you want. It starts with you. Gandhi said it best. He said, "Be the change you want to see in the world." I tell you: Be the change you want to see in your marriage. Your marriage deserves that you give it your very best.

Many times our marriages fail because we just don't know what we don't know. We're lost. We've never really been trained in how to have a good marriage. We just get married. All we've ever seen is what our parents have done. We don't know anything more than that. We wing it the entire time as we go. Winging things is okay sometimes, but when we talk about hope for your marriage you're going to have to do a lot more than just wing it if you want to get your marriage to work. There are things you are going to specifically have to do, specifically have to give up, in order to make your marriage work. There is a plan that has to be put into place for this to work.

There's hope for your marriage whether your spouse wants it or whether your spouse doesn't want it. There are many marriages saved every day when one spouse doesn't want it, because the change that you make may be exactly what is needed to bring your spouse back in, to create a new level of communication, and to create a new level of love.

You notice there's a word I use a lot. That word is create. In making any marriage work, we have to create the things we want. You say, "Well, I got married ten years ago. I was so in love with my spouse. Now, not so much." That's not so abnormal. We've just stopped creating love. Imagine this, when you were boyfriend and girlfriend, what did you do? You created love. You went out of your way. You made them a priority. You found ways to bring life to your relationship. When we talk about the hope for your marriage, there's going to be a creation factor in here where you're going to create things in your marriage and your life. You're going to do things differently, in a different way, with a different mindset and with a different thought process. When we get into Chapter 3, we're going to start really focusing on what we need to do.

I want you to see hope for your marriage. You're going to be able to make it happen. I want you to have faith in yourself. I want you to have faith in your spouse. I want you to open yourself up to fate and believe that God has given you this great ability to make this marriage work.

You say, "I've been praying every day for God to make my marriage work." Do you remember the story that's been shared many times, in many ways, about the person who is stuck out in the middle of the ocean, asking God for help? Someone comes by on a boat and throws him a life preserver. He calls back, "Oh no, I'm waiting on God to help me." Then another boat comes by a little while later and asks, "Hey, do you need help?" He goes, "Oh no, no, no, I'm waiting on God to help me." Then another boat comes by and he again calls out, "No thanks, I'm waiting on God to help me." Now the man drowns and goes to heaven, He asks God, why didn't you help me? God says I sent you three different boats.

Sometimes this is what it is in our lives. We're given an opportunity, a plan and a way to get what we want, which is help, but we don't see it as help. Or, it seems like something we don't want to do because it's not what we wanted, or it's not how we wanted it to come.

Realize that your marriage is one of the most important covenants you have gone into, one of the most important decisions you have ever made. This was a lifelong commitment. If you made a lifelong commitment, wouldn't you want to work this out and make this good? Think of all the time you spent planning this wedding. Think of all the time you spent planning the honeymoon. *How much time did you spend planning the marriage?* How much time did you spend planning how you're going to work things out as a couple? How much time did you spend planning your future goals as a couple? I guarantee you know what you want to do with your life and your business, so what about your marriage?

So, again, is there really hope for your marriage? Absolutely there is hope for your marriage. Absolutely. I'm going to teach you how to get a different mindset in Chapter 3. We'll go deep into just letting go of what's not working. Then we'll move into what is working. We're going to learn to change our focus on the things that are of value, and things that are going to bring value.

I want you to look in the mirror and I want you to say, "My marriage can work." I want you to tell yourself that every single day. Ten, twenty times a day, tell yourself, "My marriage can work." I want you to start believing in yourself, in your marriage and you. I want you to believe that you have the ability to create the best marriage ever. I want you to see yourself as that person who can create anything you want. I want you to see that you're the one who has the clay and you're forming the clay, which is your marriage, into exactly what you want it to be. You have what it takes to make your marriage work. You have what it takes to create and to have the very best marriage ever.

When you think of your marriage, I want you to think of your marriage as the smiling marriage. Tell yourself: "I think about it every day. I smile when I think about my marriage. I smile when I think about my spouse. I smile when I think about what's going to happen when they come home. I get excited, I get pumped, I get motivated because I know that I have what it takes to create and to have the best marriage ever. I can do this."

I want you to look yourself in the eye and I want you to believe in yourself. I want you to scream to yourself, "I can do this. My wife deserves it. My husband deserves it. We both deserve a great marriage together!"

Why do you want to go through your life miserable? Nobody in their right mind does. We're going to start making a phenomenal marriage; we're going to create the marriage of our dreams right now.

"I don't want to be married just to be married. I can't think of anything lonelier than spending the rest of my life with someone I can't talk to, or worse, someone I can't be silent with."

— *Mary Ann Shaffer*

If you find yourself in need of 1 on 1 marriage coaching, couples marriage coaching, or an intensive workshop, (Marriage by Design Workshop), contact us via website: **www.thesmilingmarriage.com**.

Chapter 3

Letting go of what's not working

I hope your you're looking at your marriage in a different way with a different perspective, and you're starting to see things with new light, with new hope, and with a new passion that you know that there is a hope for your marriage and you know that there is a hope for what you want to create out of your life. I wholeheartedly believe that if we follow the system, the system will lead us to great successes in our relationships. Let's make this a journey to remember. Let's make this journey so amazing that years form now, you're going to have stories to tell, your kids are going to have stories to tell, your family's going to have stories to tell, your friends are going to have stories to tell. They're going to be looking at your life and saying, "If you only knew them before." They're going to be like, "Wow, what was happened to you?" The stories are going to be amazing.

Your positive relationship changes will shine upon so many other lives. They're going to see you as their example to follow for the positive, the good, the love of your marriage, the love of your kids, the love of just humanity all by itself. You're going to change things about yourself through this program that's just going to blow people away. They're going to be excited for you, and about you. Just a warning. Some people, well, they're just going to be jealous. They're going to look at it in a negative outlook. They're going to see it in a way to where they want to bring you back down to their level because of their misery. But you'll stay above that.

I want you to stay the course no matter what you do, because remember, you're setting the example. John Maxwell always said, "A leader, he knows the way, he goes the way, and he shows the way." As you develop your relationship, you're going to become a leader amongst your friends, amongst your circles of people, amongst your circles of influence. You're going to become a leader in such a way that people are going to want to be like you. They're going to want to know, "What has happened to you?" You're going to be able to share your own story of hope about how your relationship came back to life.

#1 - Set Aside Your Problems

We're going to look at five different things that are going to help you in this chapter. Number one is going to be the most important one for you to focus on, at least for right now. And what is it? It's setting aside your problems. You're going to have to learn to set aside all the issues that you have that are creating drama, misery and error. You need to learn to set aside these problems while you focus on a new solution. That second part of that sentence is the goal: to try new solutions.

This is nothing new under the sun, understand that. There are many, many, many, many counselors and marriage coaches who are going to tell you the same thing, which you have to learn to set aside the problems so you can focus on the solutions.

Another important point: Sometimes the problem is we don't have a solution, so all we focus on is the problem. We don't know how to set aside the problem. We don't have a clue as to how to set it aside. All we see is how bad it is. All we see is that it's just not working. All we can say is, "God, why does this keep happening?"

The key to a great relationship is to first understand *what a solution is*. One of the most important things that I find in any kind of human development or success in life is to know what it is you want. When you can set aside your problems, you need to understand, first of all, what it is you want so you can focus on that and work towards it. If you just set aside your problems and you have nothing to work towards, nothing to focus on, you're going to have a giant issue when it comes to not thinking about all of the other problems. You won't have anything else to focus on, because all you have is what you've done for so many years: those behaviors, the issues, the anger, the hatred, the name-calling. I could go on and on.

Most importantly, you need something else to focus on. Set aside your problems. Look at them and just say to yourself, "I can't put them off, because they're real. They're part of my life." I agree with you. You can't. You have to understand that your problems have been created over time, and it's going to take a little bit of time to get rid of those problems and to get rid of those issues. It can be done, without a doubt. Remember this. It can be done.

Looking at your issues means you're going to acknowledge that you have a problem. You're going to acknowledge that the problems are there, but you're going to tell yourself, "Right now, I realize I have an issue. I have a problem. I have a lot of hurt. I have a lot of anger. But, because I want to make my marriage work, I'm going to change what I focus on. I'm going to set aside my problems, and I'm going to start looking at my relationship in a different way. I'm going to start looking at my relationship in a way that's going to empower it to have life. I'm going to look at my relationship in a way that's going to give me hope, because I know without a doubt it can work."

You've acknowledged that you've got a problem. Now we're going to set it aside. We're going to just put it away, put it in the closet for now, while we do something different. Remember something. The definition of insanity is, what? Is doing the same thing over and over and over, and you're expecting different results. That's not going to happen at all. If you don't set aside the problems, then you're going to have the exact same result. We have got to learn to just put things back and say, "Wait, and stop. I can't do this anymore."

#2 - Look at Your Relationship from a Different Perspective

Now that we've talked about setting aside your problems, let's talk about how to look at your relationship from a different perspective. This is so important. You have got to look at your relationship from a different perspective. You cannot keep looking at it with the same eyes you've looked at it for the last few years, or however long your relationship has been deteriorating. When we can't change what we see, it makes it hard to want to change it. All we see is the negative, and then all of our focus is on the bad and the ugly.

I'll give you an example. You could say to a person, "I want you to tell me 10 things you don't like about yourself," and just like that, they can rattle off 10 things that they dislike about themselves. "I don't like my weight. I don't like my hair. I don't like my eyes. My one finger is longer than my other finger. My one toe is longer than my other toe. One side of my butt is bigger than the other butt cheek." They can come up with a whole gamut of problems that they can share with you that they don't like about themselves. It just goes on and on when you look at the list. People focus on all these negative things, and all they see are the negatives, because their perspective is about all the bad. All they see is the bad. All they see are the things that are making them miserable.

This is where you've got to learn to change your perspective. Go back to that same thing I just told you—to rattle off 10 things that you don't like about yourself—but now tell me 10 things you love about yourself. Most people will tell you that they don't really know too much of what they like about themselves. They'll be able to list maybe one thing, sometimes up to three to four at the most, because they never look at the good. They only look at the bad. They seem to be preconditioned to only focus on the bad.

I've seen this over and over. When I give this assignment, I say, "Look, I'm going to give you one whole minute. I want you to write down 10 things you love about yourself." People struggle, they really struggle with this.

When you look in the mirror, you have to ask yourself, "What do I see? Do I see any good at all, or do I see all the flaws that society has put on me? Do I see the flaws that my partner in my relationship has put on me?" Because you know it as well as I do, in many relationships, there's name-calling. "Oh, you're so stupid. Oh, you're so fat. You're such a loser.

You're no good. You're just like your mother. You're just like your dad. Your whole family's horrible." Do you see where I'm going here? It's like, "Oh my God stop already." It's just a never-ending cycle of stupidity that comes out of our mouths. After a while, we start to believe what we hear all the time. We are being conditioned to believe what we hear about ourselves. (Did you know even negative joking affects us?) Our self-esteem drops so low that we don't know what else to do, except to believe all of the negative, because that's all we ever focus on.

When you look at your relationship from a different perspective, you're going to use a perspective of hope and love. Your relationship deserves wholeheartedly, 100 percent, for you to look at it in a different mindset, with a different way. When you are in the frame, you can't see the picture. It is time to step out of the frame and see the picture from a different perspective.

#3 - Open Yourself Up To Change

Now we've covered setting aside our problems and looking at our relationship from a different perspective. Now we're moving to the third step: opening yourself up to change.

This of course ties into Number Two because part of looking at your relationship from a different perspective is opening yourself up to change, and opening yourself up to doing something different from what you've always done.

What does that mean that we open ourselves up to change? Part of the perspective is looking at it from a different viewpoint and saying to ourselves, "Okay, look. I'm looking at it from a positive view now." Are you ready for a big change in perspective? You're going to write a list out today. You can do it now, you can do it later, but you need to do it. The list is going to say, "I'm going to look at my relationship from a different perspective. I'm going to open myself up to change." How do you do that? You need to first of all see your relationship from a different viewpoint. This is part of the change.

You're going to write down 10 things that you love about your spouse. You say, "I can't come up with 10 things I love about that man. I can't stand that man. That man is so miserable. He's so ugly. He's so pathetic. I just hate that man." In all that hate and all that anger, you still love that man, or you still love that woman. You really do, because I can tell you, if another woman was to come up and start flirting with him or her, you're going to get all jealous just like that. Don't tell me you don't have love for that individual. You're just angry right now. You're just hurt right now. All that hurt and all that anger can go away when we open ourselves up to change and a new idea. Part of that is looking at your spouse with different eyes.

I want you to think about, what could you write down about your spouse that you really like? I'll give you some ideas. I love, I absolutely love the way my spouse cooks dinner for me. She makes the most amazing dinners. Remember, this can be the smallest of things or the biggest of things when you look at writing out a list of what you love about your spouse. My wife is the best cook in the whole wide world. She makes the best meals ever.

So for your wife or your husband, is it the way they smile? Maybe they make your heart melt with their smile. Or they always pick up the kid toys. Or run errands. Or shop when you're tired. Or bring you coffee. Or maybe they handle something you don't like to mess with, like the budget or laundry or getting gas for the car. Maybe they always hug you when they come home or can smooth things over with a parent or other relative. Remember, we're looking at things from a different perspective. We're opening ourselves up to change.

Are you still stuck with your list? I'll give you more examples. I like the way my wife wears her hair. I like the way my wife comes home every day from work, and she comes straight to me. I'm the first person she'll almost always come to, and she gives me a kiss. I love the way my wife presents herself in a physical manner on a daily basis. I love the way that my wife makes herself look attractive for me. Do you see where I'm going here? I'm focusing on all the things that I like about my spouse, which is going to open me up to the change and the new perspective that's going to help me move forward in my relationship.

I get this. I get that you're hurt. You're angry. You're upset. Right now, you have nothing but hatred and negative feelings about your spouse. I get that. I've been there. I understand that so well. I also know that most spouses want to have a good relationship. Most spouses truly want to change. Sometimes they just don't know how to change. Part of this change is getting a new perspective, but more than that, is opening yourself up to change, opening yourself up to new ideas, opening yourself up to a different way of doing things.

That usually means a way that you haven't done it in many, many years.

Sometimes all we've ever seen is what our parents have taught us. Sometimes all we've seen is what our friends have shown. We go to our friends. We tell them, "Oh my God. Today, my husband, and he was just such a butt face. I don't know what he was thinking. He's so rude. He's so mean. All he does is knocks me down. He tears me down. He says stupid things to me. He says bad things to me." Then your friends look at you and say, "Oh my God, my husband does the same thing. I can't stand him." Do you see where I'm going with this cycle? As you talk so negatively about your spouse to your friends, they get on board with you, and they reinforce the negativity about your spouse. Now all of a sudden, what was just a little bit of negativity has turned into a lot of negativity. Now you're like, "God, I hate him even more," because they're reinforcing how you feel, and you're reinforcing how they feel about their spouses. It's a wicked cycle that destroys relationships.

What if you went to your friend and you told her or him, "You know what my husband did today? My husband came home with flowers. I don't know what he wanted. He may have wanted sex. He may have wanted this. I don't really know what he wanted, but he came home with flowers for me today." Or, "You know what my wife did today? She came home with a card. I couldn't believe that there was a card there, and all it said was, 'I love you.'"

What if you went to your friends and told them about the positive things? Even if it's just one little positive out of a thousand negatives, it's a building block. When you look at how they built the Pyramid, they started at the bottom, with one block. Then they kept building, they kept building, they kept building, one on top of another. They could have never got to the top of the Pyramid without having something to start with. It's a foundation.

Part of your big change is changing what you're going to do and how you're going to talk. You have to open yourself up to this new idea. Don't go run your mouth to your friends about your spouse. If you don't have something good to say about your spouse, it's probably better that you don't say it. Go see a counselor. Go see a coach. Go see a therapist. Go see a pastor. Go see someone who's going to lift you up, and give you an unbiased opinion, and help you make a better choice as far as what you say and what you do. You don't have to walk away from a meeting with someone feeling miserable and down in the dumps, and that's what happens when you badmouth your spouse to your friends. They reinforce it. When your friends tell you the negative stuff, you reinforce it for them. It's such a vicious cycle, "Oh my God, stop already," because you're not helping yourself. This is about opening yourself up to change so that we can go into step Number Four here.

#4 - Let Go of Past Issues

When you open yourself up to change, you can now let go of past issues. We talked about how Number One was setting aside your problems. Number Two was looking at your relationship from a different perspective. Number Three is opening yourself up to change. Number Four is just letting go of past issues. Seriously think about it. Letting go of your past issues. You can't change what was done yesterday. You can't change what was done a week ago. You cannot change what was done 10 years ago. You can't change any of those things. All those things are gone. You can't do anything about them.

Yet sometimes, we hold onto all those things that bring us the most misery. We hold onto those things that cause us the most heartache. Even though we know that if we let go of that, our life could be infinitely better. Even though we know that if we were to push that aside and let go and forgive, our life would be such a happier life. Our relationship could be so much happier. So much time in relationships is given to blaming, holding grudges, and not forgiving.

When you look at letting go of your past issues, I get it. It's hard sometimes. We have so much hurt and pain. We have so much anguish that we've allowed to build up in our lives. I hold no grudges against anything in my past, because it doesn't serve me. It doesn't serve me with peace, and joy, and happiness. Letting go of your past issues is going to be one of the most important things you're going to do in your relationship.

Remember, it's like this. If you were to be punched in the arm, and you had this big bruise on your arm, you know that the big bruise is there. Sometimes you're trying to put it behind you and you forget that the bruise is there, but then you might bump that arm into something, and you feel the pain because the bruise is still there. We acknowledge that it's there, but we don't focus on that anymore. We've let go of what happened, and now we're focusing on what we want to do.

Let me share a story about myself. I've seen the good, the bad, and the ugly when it comes to marriage. In fact, I have been good, I have been bad, and I have been ugly in marriage. I know what it is to be on both sides of the fence, not having any clue as to how to have a good marriage or to create a good marriage. I understand this so very much. I understand what it is to go through the divorce. I understand what it is to go through the child custody issues. I understand what it is to go through all these issues and have all this anger.

I have made it a priority in my life that no matter what happens, I don't go to bed upset. Let me share a story. The other day, I met a gentleman at the store who was almost 70 years old. He began to share these different movies he was looking at with me, telling me what he liked, what he didn't like. Then his wife walked up, and he said, "Oh, yeah. My wife and I, we've been together since we were 15 years old. We have been married for all these years."

I asked him this question. I said, "What would you contribute to be the most successful part of your marriage?

What one thing could you say about why your marriage has lasted so long? What one thing could you tell me right now that would give a marriage hope?"

He thought about it for a second and said, "You know, I think the most important thing is this, is that we forgave daily, and we never went to bed mad." They made it a priority to make up no matter what they did. They made it a priority to make their relationship good before they went to sleep. They didn't want to go to bed with bitterness or any anger left in their heart.

Think of it. You can look at what happened that day and get bitter about it or let it go. If you go to bed with it, you have to imagine it's like this. It's a seed. You've got a seed. If you plant it in the ground, now all of a sudden, when you go to sleep on it, you're watering that seed. What happens when you water a seed? When you feed it, what happens? It grows. It's going to grow like a weed. You can cut out a weed a thousand times, and the weed's going to grow back, until you kill it and you get rid of it.

The only way to do that is to truly forgive. Understand that people are human. You're human. You and your spouse both are human beings. You're not perfect. We're not perfect.

We're just normal people who have normal problems. Sometimes we don't know how to let go of the bad. All we know is what we know. Therefore, we do what we do. Understand that letting go of past issues is going to free you from so much anguish and pain. It's going to free you from the anguish that you feel every single day.

If you can just go to your spouse, whether it is your husband or your wife, and look them in the eye and say, "You know what? I'm sorry. I was wrong." Leave it at that. "I'm sorry. I was wrong." If she says something or he says something, "Oh, yes. You were wrong. Absolutely, you were wrong," just leave it at that. Let them say whatever they want to say. Let them get the anger out. On the flip side of that, too, is when someone comes to apologize to you, and they say, "Hey, look. I'm sorry. I was wrong," why don't you be the kind of person who says, "I accept your apology. I forgive you"? Understand this. They may do the same thing over and over and over and over, and come to you and apologize over and over. That's part of being a human being. That's part of learning. Sometimes the only reason they do it is because they don't know any better. They subconsciously don't know any better. Their behaviors are ingrained habits that they don't realize are sabotaging their relationship.

We're going to learn how to change those as we move forward. Remember this. Learning to forgive helps you to learn to let go of past issues. Your past issues don't have to define your future. Your future focus should define your future, not your past issues, because no matter what relationship you go to, you need to learn to let go of the past issues, and you need to learn to forgive and do it daily. Make forgiveness a daily habit of your life. Make forgiveness the most important thing you could ever do in your life. Make that a part of everything that you do, because it will free you and help you to find peace in your relationship. *Please remember just because you forgive, doesn't mean that you are required to be someone's doormat either.*

#5 – Let Patience Become your Best Friend

Are you ready for the final step? So now we've talked about setting aside your problems, looking at your relationship from a different perspective, opening yourself up to change and letting go of past issues. The final step is letting patience become your best friend. Understand this isn't going to just happen. You're going to have to learn to change things a little bit at a time.

The question's always been posed, "How do you eat an elephant?" Imagine you had an elephant put in front of you, and you're like, "Holy cow. How do I eat an elephant? I can't eat it all in one sitting. It's just not going to happen. It's this ginormous 10,000-pound object in front of me that I have to eat and swallow and get down." Sometimes our relationships are just like that. We see them as this enormous problem, and we don't really know what to do. We don't do anything because we see it as an obstacle too big to conquer. We don't have any idea, so we don't try. We just accept status quo, and we keep going with what we're doing.

This is just like the elephant. We're looking at how patience can be your best friend, how patience can become what frees you and gives you hope for the future. If you've got that elephant sitting in front of you, and it's a big old elephant. You have to look at fixing your relationship in the same way as to how you eat an elephant. It's going to take some time. You eat an elephant one bite at a time. You're not going to eat it all in one sitting, because it's too big to eat in one sitting.

Your relationship has been destroyed over all these years. It's this enormous problem that you have. Break it down into small chunks. "I'm going to work on this today. I'm going to work on that tomorrow. I'm going to work on this the next day. I'm going to work on this the next day." You're going to itemize the areas of the relationship that will give you the biggest impact, and you're going to work on those first. It's hard to work on them if you don't learn to set aside your problems. It's hard to work on them if you can't look at it from a different perspective. *If you're not willing to open yourself up to change, then no matter what you do, it's not going to work.*

Let go of your past issues and create forgiveness in your life. Forgive that person, truly forgive them, and don't hold it against them daily, but rather just say, "Look, I forgive you. Let's move forward." But, remember, you need to have something to move forward to. Like I said, what happens is, you want to move forward, but you have nothing to move forward to. You have nothing to focus on. You have nothing new to work towards, so you always go back to exactly what you've done. Remember, this is going to take a lot of patience.

I'll give you an example. Many years ago my family and I were in the Big Texan Steakhouse in Amarillo, Texas. They gave us a 72-ounce steak, a roll, a salad, shrimp, and a drink, and you have to eat it all in one hour. A 72-ounce steak is a four-and-a-half-pound steak. That's one big sucker. You get one hour to eat it.

If you're just trying to do it all at one time, this is what's going to happen to you. They put you up on the big pedestal there. Everybody in the whole restaurant can see you. Anybody in the world can see you online, because it's a live event. They have you up there in front of everybody. You have to do it in one hour, or you have to pay for it. If you do it in under an hour, it's a free meal.

See what I'm doing here? This is what happens when you try to eat the whole elephant at one time, and you don't make patience your friend, and you try to hurry the process, versus letting the process work for you.

My son was around 20 years old and in the Air Force. He was full of energy. He ate this entire meal in 59 minutes. There's no way I would have done that. What happened? As soon as the meal was over, he rejoiced, he celebrated, got his picture taken, got the t-shirt, got the name on the board, then but he went outside, and what do you think happened? It all came up. Every bit of it came up, and I know it, because he took a picture of it. Who takes a picture of their gross vomit after they eat a big old giant meal?

That's what happens in our relationships sometimes—we try to force everything, so therefore, it doesn't happen. We try to fix it all in one sitting, but it just goes back to what it was. You end up going right back to where you were. You're starving for that attention again.

An old preacher out in California had a young minister come to him who had just gone through a divorce. He was distraught. He was down. Life was falling apart for him. The young preacher began to tell him all his problems and cry about how things had gone bad and how his wife had left him for another man. Things were just falling apart. All he could see was the negative side of it. He didn't know what he was going to do.

The old preacher, Ike Terry, looked at the man, and he said, "Here, come with me." The man followed him out the door. He walked up to a fence with a gate. He looked at the gate, and he said, "You see this gate? It takes a long time to get a gate." He takes him out there to the fence. He said, "You see this fence? It takes a long time to get a fence." He took him out to the yard. "You see this big pretty yard? It takes a long time to get a yard." He walked up to a rosebush, and he tells the young man, he says, "You see these roses? I want you to pull one of the roses off the bush."

The young preacher pulled the rose off the bush, and it was one that hasn't bloomed yet. The Preacher looked, and he said, "Now I want you to take that rose, and I want you to open that rose. I want you to grab it petal by petal, and I want you to open it up." As that young man began to try to open that rose, it just began to fall apart. Every time he'd pull a petal trying to open it, the petal would fall off. No matter what he did, as he tried to open it, and he tried to force it to happen, it just continued to fall apart.

The Old Preacher looked at the young man, and he said something that I've never forgotten. He said, "If you'll just let this rose do what it does, and be patient with time, and just let it unfold, it'll turn into something beautiful."

Your relationship is going to take some patience to rebuild into something beautiful. If you'll just let it unfold and allow the five step system to work for you, and make patience your best friend, you're going to find greatness in your relationship." Work the system. Set aside your problems. Change your perspective. Open yourself up to change. Let go of your past issues and forgive. Let patience become your friend.

"The more you invest in a marriage, the more valuable it becomes." — Amy Grant

If you find yourself in need of 1 on 1 marriage coaching, couples marriage coaching, or an intensive workshop, (Marriage by Design Workshop), contact us via website: **www.thesmilingmarriage.com**.

Chapter 4

Planning a new strategy

Are you ready to put some of this into action? You're starting to understand what you need to do, and now we'll talk strategy. How do you actually do it? I want to build a foundation here because, as we go into Chapter 5, we'll start building the new marital value system. Then in Chapter 6, I'll cover the plan for your great marriage. For now, let's talk about **Five Steps** that will help you build the foundation for planning a new strategy to your marriage. Remember, you cannot just put a house on the sand, because if you do, what's going to happen? It's just going to blow away when the winds come or the waters come. We always have to set it on a foundation. When we get to Chapter 5, we're going to be building on the foundation of your new strategy.

Let's get started because I'm excited. I'm pumped. I know you are, too. I know you're excited about your marriage and the changes that are going to come to your marriage. I know that you believe and feel like great things are going to happen. I just know and believe that you and your spouse have what it takes to have a marriage that is great and amazing, one that you think about every single day.

Step #1: Recognize that you can't force change on your spouse.

You simply can't force your spouse to change. When you're forcing something on somebody and you make them do it so it fits your agenda, personality, likes and your desires, and it's not something that they naturally want to do. You're forcing them to do it, you're forcing them to be who they really aren't, what's going to happen? I can tell you what's going to happen. They're going to become pretty bitter. Eventually, they're going to become very angry. They're going to just start looking at things differently. They're going to look at you differently. They're not going to have that love and that desire left there for you, because they're going to think that all you do is manipulate them into doing what you want.

I've seen this so many times in relationships where husbands hide things from their wives because they're afraid to get in trouble. Imagine that. They're afraid to get in trouble in their own relationship and these are adults. Of course, this happens with wives too. People in many relationships begin hiding things so they won't get in trouble, and it's because they know their spouse has a different way of doing things. It might not be the right way, but a different way. A lot of that is because change is forced upon people. Then you hear a lot of this, "Don't you dare do that again. You can't do that." Seriously. We talk to our spouses like, "You cannot do that ever again. Don't you dare do that ever again! I have to do it this way. I am the only one who does it right. You need to do it like this. My mom has showed me all my life how to do this and this is the way we're going to do it." We try to force change upon the spouse. We want them to look at us differently. We want a relationship that works, but most of the time we tend to want the relationship just to work for us, the individual, not for we, the couple. *Wow!!! When I realized that I only wanted it to work for me, I realized I would be miserable all the time in the relationship. So now I had to change my approach to how what I expected in my marriage.*

When you're looking at your spouse, look at them through eyes of love, compassion and mercy. Remember, they're just as human as you are, and you don't want them forcing change upon you. Look at both sides of the coin there. You don't want them trying to force you to be somebody you're not. Give the same respect that you want.

This is where you have to understand. Should I be trying to change my spouse? The answer's no. Don't try to change your spouse because you can see how it's worked out for you so far. It doesn't work. If it does work, it works short-time, short-term. It just doesn't last.

Many a men, many a women, have made sacrifice and made changes because they were forced into it. "If you don't do this, then I will divorce you," or "If you don't do this, I'm going to end this relationship and you're going to sleep on the couch tonight." What's that really doing for you? It's not creating a good relationship. There's nothing good about that at all. That's creating bitterness, resentment, resistance and defensiveness. Stop trying to change your spouse and let's focus on a different solution. What is that solution? I thought you would never ask?

Step #2: Changing yourself first is the most important part of change when it comes to your relationship.

Everybody's heard that. Change yourself first. I've said it over and over. I want to make sure this goes in and stays in, and you think about this. Gandhi said it this way, "Be the change that you want to see." I say it, "You be the change you want to see in your relationship." If you want specific things to change, I really believe that it has to start with you. You have to start changing your attitude. You have to start looking at things differently from your perspective and open your eyes to something brand new. Don't sit there trying to change your husband or your wife when you really need to be worrying about changing yourself. Start looking at yourself in the mirror and saying, "Look, what do I need to change about me that would give me a different set of results? What new actions do I need to take right now to get a different set of results?" It starts with you taking the time to look and evaluate what you're doing every single day. This is so important.

We live in this world of auto-pilot, doing all the wrong things, not conscious and aware of what's going on, so therefore, we don't change anything. We get stuck in this mindset of, "I'm just going to do it the way I've always done it because this is all I know." We never really take the time to figure out, "Is it working and if it's not working, what can I do right now to make it better?" That has to start with you about your own life, your own personality, your own self, and your own habits.

We'll really get into habits here shortly, but it has to start with your own habits, evaluate them, and becoming aware of what you're doing. Look at your life each day and ask yourself this question, "Were the choices I made today the kind of choices that brought love to my relationship? Did they empower my relationship to a better place? Did they put us in a place to where we loved each other and enjoyed each other?"

Let me give you an example. The other day, my wife and I were sitting outside on the front porch and she had found an article online titled, "21 Things a Great Couple Should Be Able to Do." One of those things was actually sitting together, whether it be on a front porch or your couch or just by yourselves where it's just you two, and enjoying your time together, enjoying your conversation together, and actually knowing each other.

Part of that change in your own life is this: Evaluating what you're doing and asking yourself at the end of the day, "Did what I did today make a difference? Did it bring life to the relationship?" You need to make an effort to bring some life into the relationship, but you can't do it unless you become aware of what's not working.

I talked to my wife about the time we spent just sitting on the porch together, and she said, "I enjoyed that time with you because we got to know each other." More people will go through their entire life and then get to when all the kids are gone, and the empty nest syndrome hits, and all of a sudden they don't know each other. I don't want you to get that far before you realize this. I want you to start evaluating your life and what's not working, and I want you to come up with a new plan of action, but it's going to take some conscious awareness. You'll need to take the time to actually think about what's not working.

To change yourself first, you've got to think about yourself first. You've got to think about what's not working in yourself. Don't just look at the husband or the wife and say, "Oh, that's what I need to change." No. Look at yourself first and ask yourself, "Is what I'm doing bringing value to the relationship?"

This doesn't mean making dinner or taking care of the kids, vacuuming the floor, taking the trash out, mowing the lawn, doing the yard work. That isn't what I mean when I say bring value to the relationship. Bringing value to the relationship is, "What have I specifically done today for my spouse that they can recognize as something I did it for them specifically to bring value to the relationship?"

When we just say, "Well, I make him dinner all the time," or, "I make her dinner and I do the yard work," does that really tell your spouse you love them? Does it show you're doing it because you love them, or is that doing it because it's a need that you both have? The yard work's got to get done. The cooking's got to get done by someone. The cleaning's got to get done by someone. Someone's has to take the kids to school. Someone's will have to take the kids to soccer practice, baseball practice, football practice, gymnastics, and dance. Those are things that have to be done regardless. This doesn't matter who you're with. Those are still things that have to get done. Those are our human needs that we're trying to meet on a daily basis.

We need to evaluate everything in the mindset of, "Did I do anything today to bring value to my relationship and to bring value to my spouse?" That's where I want you to start looking at yourself to start changing yourself.

Step #3: "What if I change and my spouse doesn't?"

That's a good question, isn't it? "What if I change and my spouse doesn't?" The biggest thing you can take from this question is that if you change and become an amazing person and the most amazing spouse that could ever be, you only bring value to yourself in ways that you just could not imagine. There's no guarantee that your spouse is going to change if you change, but you're not changing for your spouse. You're changing for yourself. You're changing to become a better you, not so you can hopefully make your spouse change. Your change is not about forcing them to change because you changed, or you're not changing in hopes that, "Well, if I do it, they're going to do this and if they don't do it, then I'm just going to go back to what I was doing." It can't be that way at all. You've got to want to change for yourself.

I believe, wholeheartedly, that in most cases when one person changes in the relationship, other things change. It's the law of cause-and-effect. When we do something, there's a reaction to what we've done. When you're looking at changing yourself, don't get so hung up on, "what if I change and my spouse doesn't," because that's a possibility. Your spouse may not ever change. They may stay exactly who they are, but I don't believe that's possible. The reason I don't believe that's possible is because if you are doing things differently, you almost always end up with a different result.

If all you've ever done is argued, complained, griped, tore down, tore apart, and degraded, we can probably guess what kind of reaction you've gotten. What would happen if you started doing nice things, caring things, kind things? Do you think they're going to yell at you? Do you think that if you walked up to your spouse and you said, "I want you to know you are the most beautiful person ever," do you think they'd say, "Woman, you are just one ugly, old woman. You are stupid. What in the world were you thinking?" Do you think that they would talk to you that way if you had taken the time to compliment them? Do you think if you bought your wife flowers that she would come home and say, "Why in the world did you buy flowers? What's wrong with you? Are you stupid?" Seriously think about this. Do you think that they would do that? Not at all.

When we do things, we do things with the purpose of becoming better ourselves. In turn, our circumstances will almost always get better, but the change has to start with us. Don't get caught up, once again, on, "What if my spouse doesn't change?" You're changing because you need to change. In turn, almost always, you get a different reaction and result. Remember to make it fun. Find fun things that you can do in the relationship to bring about change. We're going to talk about those changes shortly in the next chapter, but right now we just want to build the foundation.

So you start changing yourself and doing things to show love. The next logical step is expecting results.

Step #4: How long should it take before I see some change?

That's Great question. It's going to take as long as it takes. There's no real answer to that question. I have to tell you, that is a million-dollar question. How long should it take before I see some change? You could see change immediately.

Instantly. Just like that. In a heartbeat. It could also take you a month to see change based on what you two have done for all the years you've been together.

I believe that change can happen immediately. When you start doing something different, it creates a different reaction, it creates a different end result. We just talked about that. You can see change instantly depending on how your attitude is.

Now, I know of spouses who, when they come home from work, the first thing they do is say, "Hey, will you take the trash out, please? Hey, will you go out and get that yard work done? Hey, will you go pick up dog poop? Hey when is dinner going to be ready?" If that's the first thing you ever hear when you walk in the door and that's the first thing you say when your spouse walks in the door, you might not feel too loved. We discussed how those are real things that need to be done, but right now you want to focus on putting life back into your marriage and showing love. If your spouse came in the house that day and you met them with a kiss and that's something you've never done, what do you think the reaction would be? Do you think it would bring some change? You may not physically see the change at that moment, but I believe inside that person would be wondering, "Oh my, what just happened? Where did this come from?" They didn't hear you nag them.

Husbands and wives, this goes for both of you. This isn't just for one or the other. You didn't nag them. You didn't say anything harsh to them. You didn't try to tell them to do something. You didn't give them an order. Rather, you gave them some value. They walked through the door, and you gave them a kiss and said, "Hey, how was your day? Hey, I missed you today." Maybe when they walked through the door, you just went up to them and gave them a hug. They say a hug that lasts for twenty seconds releases endorphins. It makes you happy. It actually kills depression. Pretty crazy, isn't it?

Change could happen instantly. All these things are real. They're very real. You may say, "Well, I've tried everything." No, you haven't. If you've tried everything, things would be different. A lot of what you tried may have been the wrong things or you had the wrong focus, so with the wrong focus you've been doing the wrong things. Remember, what you focus on gets your attention. Keep that in mind as we move on to the next step.

Step #5: Change will start with a new focus.

I'm excited about this one because this is going to go right into Chapter 5 where we will talk about you building a new marital value system. Change will start with a new focus. This is one of my favorite subjects; what we focus on is what we get. Imagine that you looked at your relationship and life, and wrote down everything that you focused on throughout the day. Then as you looked at the results, you asked yourself, "Did I get what I focused on today?" You're going to see that you are focusing on things that bring no value, things that have really nothing to do with bringing good to the relationship.

This goes for every part of your life. What we focus on is going to get our attention. If we focus on some of the smaller things that bring no value, we're going to always get that. We always go back to that saying, "The definition of insanity is doing the same thing over and over while expecting different results." If you could evaluate that and say, "What have I been focusing on? Why has it been the way it has been for so long?" You're not looking and saying, "Well, because he did this," or "she does this," or "they don't do that." That's just blame.

We're looking at focusing on understanding what's really happening. What am I really doing? What am I really saying?

You have to make an effort here to understand what's not working in the relationship. You can't just sit there telling your spouse that it was their fault. Most of what happens in the relationship is a combined effort of doing nothing. It's a combined effort of having no focus and having nothing to focus on that's worthwhile. We live in this mindset of being on autopilot. We've been trained and conditioned our entire life to be a certain person and to be one way. In a relationship, we are that person. You do things and don't even realize you do them, or understand why you do them because you are living on autopilot with all the things you've learned over the years and the behaviors and habits you've adapted. They become your everyday life and it becomes your autopilot.

I was reading in a book by biologist Bruce Lipton, a brilliant man that's written a couple of books. He said that five percent of the time is about all that we ever live being consciously aware of what we're doing. The other ninety-five percent of our time, our subconscious mind is driving the boat.

We live in this mindset of autopilot doing things that are breaking us apart, which are tearing us down. We're only five percent aware of what's going on during any given day on average. What would happen if you became more aware in your relationship? What would happen if you learned to give your relationship a new focus? What would happen if you found something worthwhile to focus on in the relationship? How different could it be?

You could change the autopilot. The only way to change an autopilot is to reprogram it. When the pilot gets on the airplane, they program the coordinates of where they're going. When they take off and get up into the air, they hit a button and guess what? Autopilot takes over. As they get off course a little bit, autopilot re-corrects. As they get off course again, autopilot re-corrects. It keeps them on the right course to get the right destination.

Part of focus is reprogramming your subconscious mind to do what you want it to do while you're in autopilot. If you're only aware of what you're doing five-to-seven percent of the time, and you're not getting the results you want, then maybe we've got to change what we're focusing on so we can change our behavior patterns, which in turn will change our subconscious behaviors.

Now this is only going to happen through repetition. You're not going to do this overnight because you spent thirty-some-odd years, depending on how old you are, on developing these habits and creating your own autopilot. You have your own autopilot for every part of your life. You can use this in any part of your life. You're going to have to learn to change what you focus on continually until it becomes a subconscious habit, a normal part of your life.

I did this. It works. I know without a doubt it works. I knew I had a bad marriage, so I changed who I was as an individual and what I focused on. I wrote down who I wanted to be and who I wanted to become, and what kind of relationship I wanted to have, and I read it over and over every single day. I watched myself change to become the exact person I wanted to be. I consciously made myself aware until it became a subconscious habit to where I was on autopilot to make my marriage good. Yours can be the same way. Remember, your marriage doesn't have to be hard at all. Your marriage can be great. It can be whatever you want it to be, but you've got to first of all understand what it is you want it to be.

"The more you invest in a marriage, the more valuable it becomes." — Amy Grant

If you find yourself in need of 1 on 1 marriage coaching, couples marriage coaching, or an intensive workshop, (Marriage by Design Workshop), contact us via website: **www.thesmilingmarriage.com**.

Chapter 5

Building a new marital value system

Congratulations on coming so far! You are truly committed to making your marriage great. Remember, nobody starts in marriage expecting it to be bad. They always have high expectations when they get married. That's one of the most exciting points, especially of a female's life, is when that guy gets down on his knee or even that girl gets down on her knee and proposes to the other individual. Man, what an exciting time that is.

I remember when I proposed to my wife. I got down on my knee with that really nice, pretty ring that we had picked out, and I proposed to her. I remember how excited she was. She wanted to tell everybody. She wanted to show off the ring. She wanted to show off how cool it was, how beautiful it was, how amazing it was. Guess what? This is where you are right now. Right at this minute, you're excited about the new changes and new growth that your marriage is going to have.

In the previous chapters, we've talked about reprogramming our mind and habits, and changing some of the things that we've done. So we're going to change those things, and part of that is completing what you started. You've already started creating new things by changing your thoughts, changing what you focus on, changing the things that have caused you heartache, and focusing on things that provide and empower greatness in your relationship.

We are going to look at building a brand new marital value system. We talked about a lot of things in the last chapter on planning a new strategy, building a foundation, about change and focus, but now it's time to really start building the new marital value system. Your value system will be built upon the foundation, and that's what we're going to do.

The 90/10 Rule

We're going to talk about to start the 90/10 rule to create immediate change in your relationship. You're probably thinking in your mind right now, well, what in the world is the 90/10 rule? Is that some kind of crazy thing he's concocted? Who knows?

But let me tell you, this is probably going to be one of the most spectacular ways you could go about creating a great life in your relationship because when you use this rule, you're going to change so much of what you do. So much of what you've done is going to change immediately. In Chapter 3, we talked about letting go of what's not working and letting go of past issues. We talked about setting aside some problems that are causing us the heartache that causes us so much pain. Well, now we're at a point where we're going to start using the 90/10 rule to get our marriage on track and to start changing the marriage immediately.

Now, when you look at most marriages and most relationships, they focus on all the bad. I could venture to say that if you were to look at a relationship, even evaluate your own and looked at what you focused on, I can almost guarantee you will say that you focus about 90% of the time on the problems, the things that cause us heartache, and the negative aspects to the relationship. You see that, you understand that, you know that. So now that you're aware of that, it's time to change the focus because we've spent so much of our time on autopilot. With autopilot, focusing on past issues, past problems, and current problems, all we focus on then is what we don't want. We always focus on what we don't like. We always focus on the things that are causing us to make bad decisions, to not do things right, to be critical, to be harsh. We tend to see all the bad versus seeing all the good, and when all you focus on is the bad, that seems to be all that you ever get.

What you focus on—that's where your intention goes. So the 90/10 rule is like this. We spend 10% of our time and never more focusing on the problems, 90% of our time focusing on the solutions to our challenges. So we're going to spend 10% of the time acknowledging and addressing any problems. Then we're going to learn to focus 90% of our energy, our efforts, our mind, our thoughts, our actions, our physical body and our words on what we want out of the relationship. What does this look like? So let me give you an idea of what this looks like for me.

For me, when I learned the value of the 90/10 focus rule, it changed my life forever. I decided what I wanted, and I focused exactly on that. You can look at the average person. They'll focus on a very specific set of goals, and they'll work very diligently towards that set of goals, accomplishing the end result with whatever goal they had set for themselves. In almost any marriage, you'll never find a goal that they've set as far as who they want to be, what they want to be, what kind of marriage they want to have, and the intention as to how they're going to do it. So when we look at the 90/10 rule, it's so important to understand that if we're going to make this marriage work, we have to stop focusing on the problems. We have to set the problems aside, and we have to start focusing on the solution.

Moving forward, 90% of our focus should be on what we want in our relationship; 10% of our focus will be on the problem. Remember, the problems do exist still. We still need to address them, but we don't want to put our focus there. So many problems go away when we change our focus. *When we change the way we see things, the things we see will change.* This isn't about he's right or she's right. This is about coming together with a common focus, with a common set of goals, with a common structure centered on creating a great relationship. Your relationship will be great. Just give it time.

Creating a Marriage Plan

I've studied goals and setting goals for a long time. I've studied people who set goals and how that can change their lives and their focus. I've watched how having a goal written down in front of them changed what they focused on every day. I've watched how having a goal has really forced them into making different decisions because they had an end outcome in mind. They got it because their focus and their actions were always geared towards the outcome. They were consciously aware of what they wanted because they looked at it daily. It is often said that a goal is not a goal until you write it down. It's only a wish or a dream until you put it in writing. I believe that because until you write it down, you can't see it, and you're probably not going to focus on it. You're going to forget about it and not do anything about it. You end up going back to the old behaviors and old patterns that did not serve you or your relationship.

We've got to create a marriage plan in such a way that it's going to get us to where we want to be. You're at point A, and you want to be at point Z, so how do we get from A to Z? That's through a marriage plan with absolute flexibility built into it. Flexibility is going to be the key. You're still going to be human when you wake up tomorrow. You're still going to make bad choices. You're still going to do things that don't please your spouse or things that make you unhappy because you didn't do the right thing, so you're angry with yourself. You're not always going to get it right, but that's okay. Be flexible when you start looking at creating your marriage plan.

Your marriage plan is going to be the key to getting what you want out of your marriage, because you're now going to become conscious and aware of what you want. Remember, we talked about how 95% of our life is spent on autopilot, ran by our subconscious mind; 5% of our time we are actually conscious and aware of what we're doing, what we're thinking about and the choices we're making. We have to become more conscious and more aware of what we want. We need to use repetition to change our subconscious patterns and our subconscious behaviors so our marriage will change directions completely.

The biggest thing is on any plan, is if you don't know where you want to go, you're more than likely to never get there. Your marriage has to have some kind of plan of action to get what you want. I've asked so many people, "What are your marriage goals? What kind of goals do you really have for your marriage? What kind of goals or plan do you have moving forward as far as making this a great marriage, not just a marriage that exists?" Most people get married, and they live on autopilot, and their marriage exists, but most marriages never really thrive because the people don't intentionally try to make it thrive. That's the problem, so we've got to create a plan. When you're going to build a house, the first thing you do is you create a plan. You think it out, you know what you want it to look like, you create a plan from start to finish, and then you start working the plan step by step. Let's get looking at what we want to do as far as our marriage plan goes.

Who You Want to Be

First we need to look at who do you want to be. You can't become someone if you don't know who it is you want to become. Pretty simple psychology, I'd say. If you wanted to become a school teacher, you became a school teacher because you knew that's what you wanted to become. You took the time to get educated in the area of being a school teacher. It's that simple. You knew, so therefore, you chose specific actions to get you where you wanted to be. So deciding who you want to be is so important to understand.

In your marriage, as a husband and as a wife, I want you to think about and decide who do you want to be? *Notice I didn't say who you want your spouse to be.* No, that's not what I said at all. We're not talking about changing them or who we want them to be, but we're talking about who I want to be as a husband, and who you want to be as a spouse. We're going to start there because that is the most important part of this.

What kind of man do you want to be? What kind of husband do you want to be?

What kind of wife do you want to be? What kind of woman do you want to be?

What does that look like to you?

So ask yourself these questions as you look at this. Most people will say, "I want to be a good husband," or "I want to be a good wife." You understand that's very vague, right?

Let's really define what that means to you when you say that you want to be a good husband or a good wife. What does that look like? Because we've all had models growing up from our mothers, our fathers, our grandmothers, our friends, our neighbors, our aunts and our uncles, but this is about you now. This is about you deciding who you want to be. This is going to be so important for you. Now, I want you to think of it this way: I want to be the kind of man who is loving. I want to be caring. I want to be kind. I want to be soft spoken. You're looking at things that you want to be as a man and as a husband. I want to be someone who values my wife. I want to be someone who opens the car door for my wife. I want to make sure I go out of my way each day to give my wife value. I want to become someone that my wife will love. So we go back to, who is that?

We're going to create who we want to become and who we want to be. I did this for myself, thinking about who I wanted to be as a man, and what I wanted to do when I came home from work. I wanted to create my reactions ahead of time. I know this sounds crazy, but I decided that if my wife got mad, I was going to react in a soft spoken voice because this is who I wanted to be. I planned to come home from work and give my wife a kiss. I planned that. I planned to buy my wife flowers. I planned to say something nice to my wife each day. I planned to buy my wife a gift every week.

I know a guy who for the last 20 years has bought his wife a gift every single week. You see, that's conscious awareness. He's already decided who he wants to be, and what he wants to do to bring value to the relationship. Now, because he decided that, he's made this happen every single week. He made his wife a priority.

I know another guy who has a great relationship with his wife. They've been married for a long time, like 30 years. Every time I see him with his wife, he always opens the door for her. He always gives her value, and always talks about how beautiful she is to her and in front of other people. This can be part of who you become, who you decide to be. I want to be someone who compliments my wife daily. So you say to yourself I'm going to write this down. I will compliment my wife daily. I will compliment my husband daily. I will do something each day to bring value to my relationship. Now, I can't give you all the examples because I don't know your personal relationship. I don't know what your personalities are, but I know that if you decide on who you want to be as a person, you can be all those things. Let's say you want to be kind, loving, caring, and soft spoken and motivated. You can be all of those things.

But most of the time we live in a subconscious autopilot mode of being mean and nasty and unkind, saying mean things, bad things, ugly things. Our kids see this, and we model that in front of them. Then they're going to take this with them when they leave the home. They're going to be on autopilot just like you are, doing the same things. So most importantly, decide who it is you want to be as a husband or wife.

What Kind of Marriage Do You Want?

Have you ever really taken the time and asked yourself, "What kind of marriage do I really want?" I mean, when you started, you started out with the intention of, "I'm going to have a great marriage. It's going to be awesome. I'm getting married for life, and it's going to be the most amazing thing ever!" And then—reality hits you in the face and now you hate her, she hates you. It's just ugly. I mean, we started with great intentions, but we never really sat down and decided what kind of marriage we wanted at all. We just knew we wanted to be married. We knew we loved the person, but this is marriage by design. Just like creating your own life, you need to decide what it is you want when it comes to your marriage.

This is where you two both can sit down together and just say, "Hey, look, this is what I want in a marriage. This is what I would like to see happen. This is how I would like it to be." Some examples may include: I'd like to go on vacation twice a year. I'd like to go on two mini-vacations twice a year. I'd like to sit on the front porch once a week with my spouse. I'd like to go on a date once a week. I'd like to go have free time and just have fun with my wife, my husband, and my kids.

See, what we're doing is we're writing down what we want our marriage to be. We're giving our marriage something to work towards and focus on to create a lasting change.

How about: I'd like to spend one evening a week watching a funny movie with my spouse. I'd like to spend one hour a week riding a bicycle with my spouse. I'd like to spend one hour a week just talking about our days. I'd like to spend five minutes a day where we sit down together as a family or just as a couple and share our wins and our losses of the day, our high points and our low points.

Do you see what I'm saying here? We're looking for you to decide what kind of marriage you want and to actually write it out. When you write it out and read it every single day, it's going to become a part of your life. Your life is going to become what you put down on paper. But there's more to it than just putting it on paper, obviously. You get that. I get that. We all get that, but it's so hard to hit a target that you can't see. You tend to forget what that target is. It's so hard to hit a target that's just not out there. I want you to realize that you can absolutely do this, but you've got to take the time to figure out who it is you want to be as a husband or wife, and what kind of marriage you both want. This is so important because it's hard to focus on a marriage that you want when you live in autopilot and past issues, and where your focus is 90% on all the problems. (Remember the 90/10 rule!)

Now, could you imagine what life would be like if you actually focused on what you wanted? This is part of designing who you want to be. You decide ahead of time that if you get mad, you are going to react in a new way, and you're going to tell that to yourself every day, 50 times a day. I don't care how many times it takes until it becomes a part of your subconscious behavior, to where it's just an instant reaction where you see it, you know it, you plan it, and you're going to do it. It doesn't have to turn ugly every single time something happens. You can learn to recreate your reactions to the problems. That all comes down to what you decide to focus on, who you decide to become, and what you decide for your marriage to become.

Creating Lasting Habits

This is going to be the most important part: creating the habit of change. No matter what you do, if you don't do this part, it's not going to stick. It'll stick for a short time while you're excited and while you're emotional about it, and then it's going to go away. It's almost like the honeymoon is over again, but we're here to create lasting change. You're going to do this for the next ten years of your life.

You've got to make it a plan and make the plan work for you, and the biggest thing is to make it a lasting habit because all of our life is being driven from the habits that we have. Every action that we have, almost every one of them, comes from our habitual behaviors that we have and the patterns that we live in. It's time to change the paradigm of what we do, so we're going to create lasting habits. You're going to write down who it is you want to be as a husband and as a wife, as a man and as a woman, what you want that to be like, who you want that to look like, what your reactions are going to be, how you're going to react to your spouse, and how you're going to react when you get mad. You're going to decide who you want to become as a person, and you're going to work on becoming that person.

Now, you've also written down what kind of marriage you actually want to have, and what you want your marriage to look like. You've really designed it in a lot of detail, but remember the key factor in this whole thing is flexibility. You have to have flexibility because you're humans and you need flexibility. It is okay if you stray off, but remember when an airplane is on autopilot and goes off course, it automatically corrects to get back on course. You can do the same thing, but you've got to have it set first. So creating this lasting habit means you've taken these goals, you've written them down of what you want yourself to be and what you want your marriage to be, and you're going to read them every single day. You're going to put them in front of you everywhere you are. You're going to have them at your desk at work. You're going to have them in your car where you can see them. You're going to have them in your house. You're going to write them on your bathroom mirror. You're going to hang them anywhere you are throughout your day as a reminder of who you want to become and what you want your marriage to be because it's going to keep your focus on the things that you want.

Your normal problems are going to be there. You're still going to have some money issues here and there. You're still going to have some kid issues. You've got to take this kid here. You've got to make dinner for this. Those are going to be the norms, but your focus as far as your relationship goes is going to be on what you want to create because you want to create an amazing relationship. Why not have a relationship that matters? So you're going to read this every single day. You've set it everywhere you could be in the entire house. Your kids have seen it. You have seen it. You're holding yourself accountable.

Now, husbands and wives, remember this. You at no point ever, ever, ever, ever, ever get to judge your spouse if they fall away from the goal. You don't get to bash them. You don't get to tear them down because remember what I talked about. Flexibility. You're human. You each are human beings susceptible to failure and making bad choices.

Now, that's no excuse to not try, but remember you're not going to get it right all the time, so we don't want to hold grudges when things don't go right. You've already decided how you're going to talk things out. We're going to have a conversation about it, and you've already decided what you're going to do, and you're going to make it work. But don't spend 90% of your time talking about the little issue that came up. Spend 10% of the time; acknowledge it and say, "Hey, look, we made a mistake. Okay. I'm sorry. You're sorry. We're both sorry. I love you. You love me. Let's make out. Let's go have a great time, and let's just get over it." There is no need to hold the grudge there. There really isn't because holding the grudge only makes you angrier, and when you're angrier all you focus on is the problem. Remember, we're focused on the solution.

The solution is who you want to become and what kind of marriage you want to create. Read your marital goals every single day. You have your personal goals of who you want to be as a person, as a man or as a woman. You have your marital goals as a couple, who you guys want to become. You guys both need to read these daily, every single day without fail. I promise you this will change things. This changed my life when I did this. It changed my marriage. It changed who I was as a man. I changed in ways I never could have dreamed because I found this system on accident and realized holy cow, where has this been all my life? I was never conscious or aware of what I wanted. Then when I decided I wanted it, I wrote down everything I wanted to do, who I wanted to become, and I read it every single day. I read it over, and I read it over, and I read it over. I read it until it became a part of my DNA, and to this day it's still a part of my DNA.

Sometimes if you get off track, you know what you do? You just go back to reading it again. You just pick it up, and you read it every day until it becomes a habitual behavior, part of your everyday life.

I know great things are going to happen in your relationship. You have already decided that you're going to change your focus. You decided you're going to create a marriage plan. You've decided you're going to decide who you want to be as an individual and as a spouse. You've decided what kind of marriage you want to have, and now you're working on creating the lasting habits by reading those goals every single day and making them a part of your everyday life. You deserve the very best marriage ever. Every single couple does. You can create it.

"Marriage is three parts love and seven parts forgiveness of sins." ~Langdon Mitchell

If you find yourself in need of 1 on 1 marriage coaching, couples marriage coaching, or an intensive workshop, (Marriage by Design Workshop), contact us via website: **www.thesmilingmarriage.com**.

Chapter 6

Working the plan for a great marriage

You're now putting in the work to make your marriage better. That means that when you look in the mirror, you see someone who is committed to making their relationship work. How exciting is that? Doesn't that just get you pumped? And get you excited about looking in the mirror and saying, "My relationship's getting better. It's finally moving in the direction I want it to go!" It starts with a commitment. You committed this far, and now you're in Chapter 6.

There's something to lifting your own self esteem out of the pits, and you're going to do it by celebrating every little success that you have. This is a great big success, and it's going to propel you to the next success. Success builds upon success. Tell yourself every day how awesome you really are. Build your own self-esteem, because as you build yours, you're going to build your spouse's. You're going to start feeling so empowered and alive inside that no matter what happens, you are excited about living. When you love yourself it's so much easier to love your spouse. Did you hear that?

When you love yourself it's so much easier to love your spouse, so get excited. Come on guys, let's get pumped, let's get motivated, let's get moving, and let's make great things happen. Pretty exciting isn't it? You get the choice. You get the choice today to make your life great.

We're going to go through five items in this chapter to help you make a great marriage plan, and number one is making your relationship come first.

#1 - Make Your Relationship Come First

Think about that: making your relationship come first. Giving your relationship some priority. Giving your relationship the kind of priority that gives it value.

In most households everything else comes first over the relationship. What does that look like? Your work can come first over the relationship. Now, we're talking about priorities here. Your kids can come first over the relationship. Sports and other events can come first over the relationship. I was talking to a lady at the dentist, and she told me, "My husband, or my fiancé rather, all his waking time is spent playing sports and having fun when he has nothing else to do."

We look at building relationships and prioritizing the husband and wife relationship, because if you don't, someone or something else going to get the attention, leaving your marriage lacking. So how do you make your relationship come first? You need to first become aware that you're not making it come first. Start looking and evaluating your life and asking yourself, "Am I giving my spouse attention? Am I giving my spouse the time they need so that we can have a positive relationship, where we have positive outcomes, so at the end of each day we're excited to go to bed together?"

Do you make time for your spouse? Or does all of your time go to the kids? You go to soccer, you go to football practice, you go to baseball practice, you go to gymnastics, and you go to dance. You'll do everything in the world for the kids, and there's nothing wrong with this, but you forget to prioritize you and your husband, or your wife. You forget to prioritize what's important, and that's your marital relationship, because all those things are fine and dandy when you're giving them priority. Your kids and their events are great, but if the marital relationship falls apart all those might just go away.

You may not be able to afford to do them anymore. Your kids' lives are going to be turned upside down. Let's focus on making your relationship come first. Creating priorities in your life right now, today, to make it happen. Let me just give you a short list of some things that you can do. First off, become aware that you're not making it a priority, and make a decision to make your relationship a new priority. Make it the kind of priority that each day you have committed to doing something good for your spouse. Make your marriage a priority by planning a weekly date. You say, "Well, I can't afford it. I don't have any money. It's too expensive. We just don't have it in our budget to go out on a date." Well, that's where we're wrong, because a date doesn't have to be about spending money. A date can be just going on a walk.

You can make time just to go on a walk with your spouse, and at this time put your phones away, and you can talk and have communication. Get to know each other, talk about your day, talk about what happened, talk about the good, talk about the bad, talk about the ugly. Talk about what was funny or share a joke you heard from somebody else. Just do something while you're out to talk to each other. Make it a fun time. It doesn't have to be spending money. You could go to a movie.

Now, a movie doesn't cost much. You could go to a movie for about twenty bucks, go to a matinee, but you're spending some time together.

You're holding hands at the theater. Yeah, don't tell me you didn't do that before. You're making out back there in the back row. Come on now, I know you guys do this too. You guys make out back there. Don't let us catch you though! But have fun. Just go to a movie, hold hands, eat popcorn together, and share a drink. Just make it priority that you are having time for yourselves as a couple.

You could go to a concert. They have a lot of free concerts many places that you can go to at community centers. When's the last time you sat in a park and just looked at each other? When's the last time you just held each other and hugged each other, and just kissed?

You can go fishing with your spouse. Out to dinner. To an art gallery. A local event. Make a date night a priority, because your kid's soccer practice becomes a weekly priority, and their game becomes a weekly priority. You say, "Well, I don't want to spend that much time with my spouse." You can make time.

Well let me tell you something, if you don't want to spend that much time with your spouse, you're going to have a challenge when your kids leave, because you might actually like your spouse if you got to know your spouse on more of a personal level. When you were boyfriend and girlfriend, you went out of your way to make him or her a priority. You went out of your way to come together to make that relationship great. You made it an absolute priority to make it a great relationship.

You can get right back to doing that. You can do it, but you have to give it some priority, and you have to do the things that are going to help you get there.

#2 - Developing the Habit of Love

Wow, what is the habit of love? What is love? Everybody's got an opinion of what they think love is. Love is kind, compassionate, forgiveness. There are so many factors we can look at when we talk about love. It's something you practice every single day. Love is unconditional. Love is pure, love is honest, and love is holy. Love is something that we all desire and want so much, yet sometimes we find so little time to give it.

When you look at developing the habit of love, it's the habit of working the plan of a great marriage. I'm going to be kind to my spouse. I'm going to show love to my spouse. I'm going to make it an absolute priority today to do something nice for my spouse. I'm going to tell my spouse something nice about them. When my wife walks out, and she looks good in that pretty dress she's got on, I'm going to look at her and say, "You look beautiful today." Or you can be like me and say, "Dang, girl, you look good." You just need to put your personality into it.

When your husband walks down the stairs looking nice, and he hasn't dressed up in a while, and you're thinking, "Man, he sure looks hot. I love that man." Tell him. Go out of your way to tell your spouse that they look good. This is the habit of love. When you see your wife standing there in the kitchen, maybe she's cooking dinner, just walk up behind her and put your hand on her shoulder. Walk up behind her, and just rub your hand through her hair. Walk up behind her, and maybe squeeze her butt. She might smack you, but hey, it's worth a try.

It's the same with your husband, ladies. Go out of your way for your husbands. If your husband is just sitting there, walk up next to him and sit next to him and say, "Hey, do you mind if I sit here and watch this television show with you?" Just sit next to him, and maybe put your hand on his leg. This is developing the daily habit of love. We're going out of our way to do nice things for our spouse. Guys if you're outside pick a flower and bring it in and say, "Hey, I was thinking about you." Ladies, leave a little card under his pillow or in his lunch. There are so many things we can do to create the habit of love. When you were a boyfriend and girlfriend, you did so many things differently, and your relationship was so different. It was exciting, it was fun, you loved it so much, but right now you've just gotten away from making your relationship a conscious priority.

Go on a great vacation together. Think about it, when most couples go on vacation, and especially if they go by themselves, they have a great time. You talk, you have fun, you sit out on the beach, you swim together, and you go to dinner. Look at the life you're living. Why can't your everyday life be like a vacation? Why can't it be?

The difference between vacation and everyday life is that on vacation you've made it a priority to have fun. You've made it a priority to live a great life. You've made it a priority to enjoy time together, so why can't you do it while you're at home? Make it a priority to have a great time, and to have a great life. You'll spend weeks and months planning that vacation, so spend weeks and months planning how great your marriage is going to be, but do it on a daily basis.

The smiles will be there in your marriage. Your marriage is going to smile; your kids are going to smile. Don't be so serious all the time about the relationship. Make it fun, be silly. If you've got to crack an egg on his head and take off running, do it. Imagine that you're cooking, and you just have an apron on. He's going to be like, "Holy cow Batman, what just happened?"

Remember we're only five percent consciously aware of what we're doing on a daily basis, and ninety-five percent of our time we're in autopilot. Our subconscious mind and behaviors are driving us. I want you to start making the habit of love a priority, so that it becomes a subconscious habit. You're going to make developing love a habit. This is just looking at some things you can do, and thinking in your mind, being aware every day, every week, every month, and every year. This is so important. Develop the habit of love, and it's going to walk with you every single day.

#3 - Working the Habit of Love – Taking Ownership

Life is too short to live it upset or unhappy. It's all a choice that we have, and we have that choice today. We have the choice to work the habit of love. We've decided we're going to do it daily, weekly, monthly, yearly. Working the habit of love is practicing what we've decided we wanted to do. When you work the habit of love, it becomes automatic all the time.

When I'd buy my wife flowers and send them to her at work, her friends would always say to her, "Can you please have your husband talk to my husband so he'll send me some flowers? Can you please tell him just to come say something to him?" Guys, when you work the habit of love it creates not just change in yourself, but it creates envy in others. They want what you have. They all of a sudden see that your life is different in so many ways, and they desire to have what you have. So many people don't get these great privileges. You be the person, and you be the couple that decides that your relationship matters.

Stop focusing on all the things that make you upset and mad. That's not working the habit of love. When all you can focus on is the things he does wrong or she does wrong, that's not working the habit of love. I'm telling you, work the habit of love. Look for positive things every day in your spouse. Find something good to say about them every day—that's working the habit of love. You're looking and being intentional about what you want to find in the relationship. You're trying to find something good. You're trying to find something powerful.

You're trying to give your relationship new life, and you're trying to do it every single day. It's a challenge when you start working the habit of love, because everything within you wants to resist, because it hasn't done this for years. I can assure you, your spouse probably loves you, loves you dearly, but so many times we just get stuck in these ruts. We really don't know what to do, so all we do is what we know, and what we know is typically just to focus on the ugly. We focus on all the little things that have upset us, and do you realize most arguments are absolutely petty? They're petty, they're meaningless, and they're over our pride.

If you get into an argument, just look at your spouse. Be the first person to step up and do it. Guys, you do it. I'm a man, so I tell you from a man's perspective, stand up and say,

"Hey look, you know what? I was wrong, I'm sorry. I apologize, I'll try not to do it," and if she starts bickering say, "Look, you know what? You're right, you're right. I was wrong, I'm sorry." Ladies, do the same thing. Just step up and take ownership of your own attitude. That's working the habit of love: taking ownership of your own attitude, because your attitude is going to determine your altitude in your relationship. Take ownership of it. Do not sit there blaming, because it is you who is responsible for what you say and your attitude. That's working the habit of love. Make love a priority in your relationship.

One of the biggest myths is that when you get married; guess what, the sex stops. No, that's not the case at all. The sex doesn't stop. You know what stops? All the things that caused you to get the sex. That's what stopped. On both sides, ladies and men, because when you were a boyfriend and girlfriend you worked the habit of love, and you weren't even aware of it. The sex was there... It was never ending. You were in the elevator; you were in the dressing room, wherever it was.

The reality is this. When you work the habit of love, the sex just keeps on going. You're going to have so much of it men that you're going to tell her, "Can't you just hold me tonight honey?" She's going to look at you like, "What?" She's going to give it to you so much, because you're working the habit of love. It's the law of reciprocation. When you do something for somebody, they want to reciprocate. Work the habit of love and all these things that you lack will come back.

#4 - Sitting Next to the Fireplace

Let me share a story I call sitting next to the fireplace. Imagine it's nice and cold outside, with snow on the ground, snow all over the trees, and the snow's still coming down. You walk over to the fireplace and said, "Hey, I'm going to get warm." Then you look into the fireplace and say, "Wait a minute, it's not giving me any heat. What in the world's wrong with this thing?" You realize, there's nothing in there. There's no wood in there, there's no gas in there, there's nothing in there to give me any heat. There's no fire.

You say, "Okay, all right, all right, I'll put some wood in there," so you go outside and grab some wood. You bring it back in, you throw it in the fireplace and you sit back down like, "Yeah, now I'm going to get warm," but you're still sitting there wondering where the heat is.

Husbands and Wives, it's the most important thing I can tell you about this. Our relationships are just like a fireplace. We can expect things out of it, but you don't get anything out of it until you put something into it. I'm really sorry, but this is the way it works. You don't get any heat out of that fireplace until you put something into it.

Now you're at a point where you have the wood in the fireplace, but it's just not enough. Just not enough to get what he wants, some heat. There's some simple ingredients that need to go into this, some simple tasks that need to go into this to get what he needs here, and your relationship is the same way. When you're making your relationship come first, and developing the habit of love and working the habit of love, this is all about putting wood in the fire. Now all of a sudden we're going to take a match, and we're going to light that fire. What just happened?

It begins to smoke, and you see the smoke coming up from where you just lit the fire. Your relationship's the same way. When you start doing these things, you're going to see some smoke. Now, all of a sudden, you're starting to feel a little bit of heat coming out of that fireplace. You're starting to feel like there's a little spark that just caught a couple little parts of the log on fire, and then as you give it some breath, and you begin to blow on that fire, you begin to give it some air, you begin to give it some attention. All of a sudden now it's starting to flame up.

Your relationship is the same way. When you start working the system of making it a priority, and making it work for you versus against you, all of a sudden it's going to be on fire. It's going to be on fire in ways you never imagined. Women, you're going to be like, "Holy cow, this is the man I married. This is the man I fell in love with." Men, you're going to think, "This is the woman I fell in love with." I mean it is the most amazing thing ever, but let me warn you, the fire will go out if you don't continue to add fuel to it. The fuel in your relationship is going to be practicing your actions of love and making your marriage a priority.

You have to make love a priority in your relationship. You got to make being aware of what you're doing a priority in your relationship, because remember that fire's going to go out. When that fire goes out, it's up to you to keep flaming it to make sure it stays lit. Ladies and men, this goes for both of you. You both need to make it a priority when it comes to your relationship, because your relationship absolutely matters. It's going to be amazing, because you're going to continue to put wood in that fire, and it's going to continue to burn.

It's going to burn bright, and it's going to bring so much heat and warmth into your lives. You're going to be so excited every single day when you wake up in the morning like, "Do you know who I just woke up to? I just woke up to my best friend. I just woke up to that guy." Or, "That gal, that I love so much, and I love so dearly." This will happen when you keep putting fuel in the fire. It's a continual thing to do every single day. Your relationship has got to matter if you want it to be great.

#5 - Making Love Last

What are you committed to do today, right now, to make your love last? Think to yourself, "I'm going to focus on what I want, which is making love last, and making my relationship amazing."

One of the best ways you can make love last is always being aware of what you've done right in the day, what you've done wrong. Evaluate your day at the end of each day. Look and see and ask yourself and ask your husband say, "Hey honey, did I meet your needs today?" Ask your spouse if you met their needs. This is communication 101. When you both get in bed together, make going to bed a priority. This is called making love last. When you go to bed together it brings togetherness. Is that crazy? Together and togetherness, but when you go to bed together it really makes a huge difference. Men and ladies, please remember this, part of making love last is giving of yourself to your spouse.

I know you can be tired at times. I know you've had a long day. You've had a hard day, but making sex a priority in your life is an absolute must. Men, this isn't just a wham bam thank you ma'am kind of thing, this is taking care of your wife too. You have to build that fire. Don't just expect her to satisfy you and then you're like, "Okay, okay, good. Thank you very much. Okay, I'm going to sleep." No, it doesn't work that way. Take care of your wife as well. Part of making love last is doing the things that bring you together, and doing the things that brings value to the relationship. It's about doing the things that make you both happy.

You have what it takes to do this. You have what it takes to make your relationship good. I've always said there is no such thing as a bad person, there's only people who make bad choices. We don't have to continue down the road we're going down. If you would just work on your relationship, and make it a priority, I promise you, you can see a difference. Learn to forgive quickly. Don't hold grudges. Don't go to bed mad. Suck up your pride. I'm telling you ladies and men, suck up your pride, get rid of it, put it aside, and don't go to bed mad. Just say, "Hey, know what? I'm sorry, I was wrong." Just suck it up and say it.

If one doesn't want to say it, the other one should just say, "Hey look, you know what? For the sake of us having love and a relationship, I am sorry. I'm sorry if I did something that offended you." Make love last in the relationship. You got to do this, this is so important. You deserve to go to sleep every night with a smile on your face, lying next to the person you love. The grass is never going to be greener on the other side. If you run off to find somebody else, I promise you the grass is not greener. The grass is greener always where you water it. Make your relationship matter, make it a priority, and let's make love last.

"The most successful marriages are those where both husband and wife seek to build the self-esteem of the other."
~Dr. James Dobson

If you find yourself in need of 1 on 1 marriage coaching, couples marriage coaching, or an intensive workshop, (Marriage by Design Workshop), contact us via website: **www.thesmilingmarriage.com**.

Chapter 7

Affair proofing your marriage

Extramarital affairs happen every day. They happen every day in homes all across the world, but I believe most of them happen because we allow ourselves to be put into circumstances that will cause us to stray away from our own relationship. Even in the worst relationships, you can affair-proof your marriage. You just have to decide today that making sure you do not cheat on your spouse is going to become an absolute priority in your life.

In this chapter, we're going to look at four different areas to affair proof your marriage:

#1 - Keeping trust alive in your marriage (or rebuilding trust)

#2 - Signs to look for

#3 - Preventing your own affair, and

#4 - Preventing your spouse's affair

I believe each one of these is significant in regards to making sure you keep your marriage affair-proof. There's no

100% solution when it comes to making sure your spouse does not have an affair. Lastly, we'll talk about how to keep your relationship alive and thriving.

Keeping Trust Alive in your Marriage (or rebuilding trust)

We're going to start talking about building trust and keeping trust alive in the marriage. When you look at building trust, it's almost always established already when you first get together. There's no reason to distrust an individual unless they've given you a reason. In most cases, when you get married there's no reason to distrust the other person. But there are those times when you get married and you've already been in a relationship where cheating was prevalent. Maybe you've had your significant other or spouse cheat on you, therefore, you come in this new relationship and you carry those feelings of distrust and wondering if your new spouse is going to cheat on you.

You have that little nagging feeling in the back of your head. That's common. It's not an uncommon thing to have that. It's just part of life. We have a responsibility, and that's to build trust in the relationship. We build trust in the relationship through time. If you start the relationship where there's trust already established, now the goal is to keep that trust. But if you start the relationship and you feel distrust because of your own past experiences, or maybe some past experiences of your spouse that you know about, or even something that already happened between the two of you, now you're going to have to build the trust.

You're going to have to keep the trust and/or build the trust. When you look at building the trust in your life, it's going to take a little bit of time. Keeping the trust takes time. They both take time to do. It's easier to keep the trust than it is to rebuild because once you lose trust, it's harder to establish that and to make sure that other person trusts you.

When you look at an affair in a relationship, don't see it as an end-all, because you're human. Allow yourself some grace. Allow your spouse some grace, and understand that we're all human. We make bad choices, but also understand that you have the right at that very time in your life if an affair does happen, to say, "Hey, look. I'm sorry. It's over." Or if you're going to keep the relationship alive to rebuild trust, then you're going to have to be willing to forgive that individual.

One of the biggest ways to keeping trust in a relationship is not allowing yourself in any situation that could cause your spouse to think that you're doing something wrong in regards to an extramarital affair. This is just keeping your wits about you and knowing your triggers, knowing the things that could cause you to fall. Understand there are many people who said, "I would never ever do this, ever." But that's never really the case. Some people will cross the line. It just happens.

When you think about keeping and building the trust in your relationship, you've just got to make it a priority that you're going to do specific things and avoid specific things. If you are one who likes to flirt, you know you like to flirt, and then you may not want to go out to a club without your spouse, because when you mix alcohol and flirting together, we open ourselves up to a behavior that we may regret in the future.

This isn't that you went out with the intent to have an affair, by no means at all. It's just we allow ourselves into positions where a nice girl or a nice boy could come up to you and say something very nice and make you feel special, and it creates all these feelings and these emotions inside of you, and now all of a sudden you may end up finding yourself in bed with this individual.

These are kinds of things you need to look for to make sure you keep the trust in a relationship. Don't allow yourself in situations to where your spouse is going to wonder and worry. Be open with your communication. Be open with what you're doing, and don't hide anything from your spouse. Have an open line of communication, and this will help keep that trust alive.

If you have to rebuild the trust, it takes time. Understand that you're going to have a lot of hoops to jump through to make sure you rebuild that trust. Don't put yourself in a position, once again, that's going to make your spouse wonder. If you've got your phone in your hand and your spouse walks up and you all of a sudden turn it off, that's probably going to make them wonder. If you got your email open, and you turn it off when your spouse walks up, it's probably going to make him or her wonder. I'm not trying to make you paranoid by no means at all, but I'm trying to help you understand that you want to make sure that you do things that keep the trust, do things that build the trust, and don't do things that tear the trust down.

There are so many reasons people cheat. People cheat for emotional needs because they want them to be met. People cheat just for the thrill of having sex with somebody else. People cheat because they just don't have any aliveness in their own marriage. They cheat because they get bored and they want more.

The number one thing we need to do is make sure that we're doing everything that we can to avoid that affair and make sure we keep that trust with our spouse, because when we avoid those things that cause affairs, you keep trust in the relationship.

When another person of the opposite sex walks up to you, make sure you introduce them. "Hey, I'm Joe. This is my wife." Make sure you introduce your wife to the other individual as your wife. Make sure people know that you're married. If you have a ring, wear your ring. Make sure people know that you're married. Do everything you can to keep that trust alive in your relationship.

Don't let your wife see you out and about with the guys or the gals without your ring on. That's a big telltale sign that you're trying to hide something or you have an ulterior motive in your spouse's mind. We're talking about keeping that trust alive. If you want them to trust you, do things that will allow them to trust you. Don't find yourself going out to places where these bad things constantly happen. Keep yourself aware of what's going on.

Know your triggers. Know your weaknesses when it comes to the opposite sex. If you know you have a weakness of a specific style, a specific area, avoid those places, because you're going to want to make sure you keep that trust alive. Your spouse may know that you have those weaknesses, and if they see that you're out doing things that could harm the relationship; they're going to probably lose trust in you. Then when you lose trust, it creates so many more issues. Then if you end up having an affair, there are so many things that could happen. Your family's torn apart. Your spouse can go have an affair just out of revenge. Avoid those things that cause the extramarital affairs. Avoid those people who cause the extramarital affairs. Avoid that man or woman who constantly flirts with you. Tell them straight up, "I am married." Keep the trust alive. You keep it. You build it. You just work on it on a daily basis to make sure your spouse believes in you, that they trust you, and that they know without a doubt you're going to be there for them.

Signs to Look For

There are some signs to look for in a marriage, in a relationship, when it comes to wondering whether your spouse is cheating. I go back to ... I don't want to make you paranoid. I don't want to make you feel all of a sudden I've got to wonder what my spouse is doing. Oh, I'd better go check their phone. Oh, I'd better check their text messages. I get the phone bill and I'd better look at everything. You might just drive yourself nuts worrying about something that's not even happening at all.

There are some simple signs you can look for, and while this isn't rocket science, there are certain things that we look for in a relationship when it comes to extramarital affairs. One of the biggest things is if your spouse comes home every day and they've lived in the same routine for a long time, and all of a sudden you see this sudden change in behavior patterns. You notice a sudden change in the behavior patterns as they're doing things differently. They're suddenly making themselves look really nice. They're getting dressed up every time they go somewhere now. They're wearing a brand new kind of cologne or a brand new perfume. You see this little pep in their step that you've never seen before, and it's not coming towards you. You see them having to stay at work a little bit later. You catch those telling little white lies. You find that maybe they're out drinking more than they used to do, or maybe they've taken a lack of interest in you. They don't have the same communication.

When you're out and about together, you see them always looking at other women, or they're always looking at other men. You see that they've maybe opened up a brand new email account that you've never seen before. We need to understand, that these are just simple signs to look for in the relationship. This isn't to make you wonder and make you worry, but these are things that you should at least look for and pay attention to, and don't be so naïve and think that this could never happen to your relationship, because it can happen to your relationship. It could happen to anyone's relationship.

Remember, you're a human being. You have feelings. You have emotions and possibly needs that aren't being met. You have sexual needs that possibly aren't being met. When you look at your spouse, look at them with eyes of love and eyes of compassion, but also understand that there may be these other things that are causing you to wonder and have this gut feeling that your spouse is cheating.

If you think they are, just go ask. Confront them. Say, "Hey, look. I'm not trying to be untrustworthy. I'm not trying to be someone who doesn't trust you. I just have this feeling that maybe something more is going on that I don't know about. I just have this feeling that maybe you may be seeing somebody else." Open that line of communication up and see where it goes. You have that right to know. This is part of being a married couple; you have the right to know and understand if there's something going on.

A lot of times, you'll be able to tell very quickly whether they're cheating or not. You're going to know within yourself, in most cases, whether they are by their response, because you've lived with them long enough that you know what the normal responses are too hard questions like this. Many times they may get defensive. Many times they may not get defensive at all. At least ask. At least take the time to ask, because they may be having an affair and maybe they want to tell you, but they're scared to tell you.

When you look for these signs, it could be an opportunity for you to confront the issue, and more than that, for them to come clean on the issue. Then you can move forward in deciding how you're going to make your relationship work and either rebuild the trust or end the relationship, but at least open the line of communication and keep it open so that it doesn't ever get this far.

I don't want you to live a paranoid life wondering whether your spouse is going to cheat or not. I do want you to live a life of being aware of your marriage, aware of how the relationship is going, aware of whether you're doing the things that you need to be doing as a spouse to make sure that you're preventing an affair. Look for those things where normal behaviors turn into abnormal behaviors that you're just not used to seeing such as a big weight loss or a big change just in their demeanor. These don't mean your spouse is having an affair, but they could. So many things can be signs, and just become aware of it. If you think your spouse is cheating, like I said, ask, but also make sure you're doing what you can to prevent an affair.

Preventing Your Own Affair

Keep yourself out of situations that would cause you to have an affair. If you're a man, don't go around women if you're by yourself, if you can avoid it. Keep yourself away from lonely women. Don't open yourself up to being someone's talk-buddy. "Well, she's just talking to me," or "He's just talking to me." It can be dangerous when you have to say, "We're just friends." Then what happens is, she begins to share all of her own personal marital issues with you and you become her confidante. He begins to share his personal marital issues with you and you become his confidante. You guys all of a sudden begin sharing all this information with someone from the opposite sex, and you start building this relationship not even realizing what you're doing. You may not even see what's about to happen or what could happen. You're opening yourself up to possibly having an affair.

You say, "Well, I would never do this. She's just my friend." Or, "I would never do that. He's just my friend." You're right. You may never do it, but you've created an opportunity to do it. You've got this person who you've created this connection with, you created this emotional relationship with. You may think, "It's just texting," but that can create a false intimacy and be very damaging to your relationship with your spouse.

You need to make sure that in order to prevent your own affair, you don't allow yourself into these situations. Because what happens is when you start sharing your information with the opposite sex, they'll start agreeing with you. They'll start validating you. They'll start giving you value, "Oh no, no, no. You're just an amazing woman. Please don't think that." Or, "I know your husband may not think you're beautiful, but I think you're beautiful."

There may be no harm intended, but then again, men aren't stupid and neither are women. If they see you're hurting and they're lacking somewhere, hey, they may take advantage of that. "Well, hey, if she doesn't want to take care of you, I sure will."

Let me tell you this. In preventing your own affair, remember this. If you're not nice to her, if you're not nice to him, somebody else will be. You've got to make sure that to prevent your own affair from happening, that you avoid those things and those people and sharing stories about your life at all costs. Go to a professional. If you need to share your personal marital issues where your marriage is falling apart, go see your pastor. Go see someone who's going to give you an unbiased professional opinion to make sure that you're not giving the wrong person the opportunity to create an affair with you.

It doesn't usually start just out of the fact of wanting to have an affair, but then there are those times when they just want to have sex. Bottom line is they're not getting the kind of sex they want in their relationship, so they go find sex somewhere else, but in most cases it's going to be an emotionally charged event. Yes, even on the man's side. That man wants to feel validated. He wants to feel special.

Remember, when he comes home or she comes home, all you have is the norm. He does his thing. You do your thing. The kids are there, and life is normal. You tell him what you want him to do, such as pick up your clothes off the floor. He tells you, I don't want to do it. He tells you, why don't you cook my dinner? And it goes on and on and on. It can be both ways. But it's the same old thing every single day. There's no real value given in the home. He doesn't feel validated. She doesn't feel validated. She doesn't feel valued. He doesn't feel valued.

This is the vicious cycle inside the home. All of a sudden, you're sharing all of your emotional drama with someone of the opposite sex, maybe at work or a friend. They make you feel validated. But when you go to a counselor, therapist or marriage coach, or pastor, they're going to make you feel validated but in a very different way. They're not going at this with the intent of making something bad happen or to have an affair with you. They're going at this with the intent of helping you work through your issues and become a better spouse and to find a solution to your possible problem that you may actually have.

Think of it like a fence. You've got to put a fence up around your relationship, a fence that protects you and your relationship from the affair. Identify those areas where you're weak and avoid them. Let's say you find yourself being around women, who get you excited, and your whole attitude is just different around them, and you want more than just what you have in your mind. It just starts in your mind. You want more than what you have in your mind and it starts there. You look at another woman and you wonder, "Man, I'd like to have her," or as a woman you look at another man and you're thinking to yourself, "Man, I'd like to have him." You need to avoid those situations where you're actually together alone. Don't put yourself in a position where you can fall. Prevent your own affair. Your affair can be prevented by taking precautionary actions. You don't have to allow it to happen. You have that ability to keep your relationship alive.

Preventing Your Spouse's Affair

The simplest way to keep your spouse from having an affair is keep your own relationship alive. Do whatever you can to keep your relationship alive. Meet their emotional needs. Meet their physical needs. If you don't know what their emotional needs are, ask them. Say, "Hey, babe, I want to make sure I'm doing everything I can to meet your emotional needs. I want to make sure that I'm doing what I can to make sure you feel valued. Are there some areas that I'm not doing well in? Is there something else I can do for you? Are there things that you would love to have from me as your husband or your wife?" Make sure you ask these questions, because by asking these questions you'll get some good answers as to what you can do.

Once you find out, get to it. You can't put this off, because they told you, "Hey, I need this." Giving value daily to your spouse is a must. You have to give them value. You've got to be nice to them. You need to love them. You need to cherish them. We need to treat them well because, remember, if you don't treat them well, somebody else will. Somebody else is out there waiting right now to treat your spouse better than you do. It may not last. They may fall into an affair and it may not last at all, but they were treated well, and that's what caused them to want to fall away. That's what caused them to want to have that extramarital relationship. It wasn't the fact that they didn't love you. They just wanted to feel valued. They wanted to feel loved. They wanted to feel alive in the marriage.

You've got to keep your sex life alive. Ladies, I know men seem to be driven just by sex, but they're not just driven by sex, they've driven by emotional needs as well. They want to feel validated.

Men, your wives like to have sex, even though you may not think so. They do. They really do. But there are specific things that we need to do to make sure we're taking care of our wives' needs, and not just wanting sex. This is an important subject.

Ladies, let me say it to you like this. If you don't have sex with your husband, somebody else will. Men, let me put it to you like this. If you don't have sex with your wife, somebody else will. There's always somebody else out there waiting for this to happen. Ladies, if you don't value your husband, somebody else will. Men, if you don't value your wife, somebody else will.

I think I made this very clear that you've got to make valuing your spouse and absolute priority, because if you don't, we are creating the circumstances for our spouses to want to have an affair. We don't want that to happen. We want to have a great relationship. We don't want to have the heartache of watching our spouse be with somebody else, and have that visual in our mind all the time. We don't want to see that at all, so the biggest thing to prevent your spouse from having an affair is to go out of our way to be the very best spouse you can be. Go out of your way to continually, constantly, always give your spouse value and treat them like the king or queen they are.

Keeping Your Relationship Alive

You can't just go about a relationship and hope that it works. You've got to put something into it. You really do. I talked to a guy a while back. The guy was telling me, "My wife won't have sex with me at all." I said, "Well, when's the last time you bought her flowers? When's the last time you did something nice for her?" His comment was this: "Well, I'm not doing anything for that woman until she gives me sex." Wow. This is two heads battling against each other. One wants this, one wants that. Someone's got to suck it up and do something differently. In my opinion, it was the man. Go and do something nice for your wife and do it on a continual basis, and you'll have more sex than you could ever dream of.

We need to really work on keeping our relationship alive, and you keep it alive by giving it value and making it a priority. You want to prevent your spouse from going to somebody else. You get pissed off if someone else is nice to her or someone else is nice to him, but yet you're not nice to him, and you're not nice to her. Give what you want. If you want them to be nice to you, be nice to them, but do it expecting nothing in return.

Show your spouse the value they deserve. That's why I believe having goals for your relationship is so important. You're working together with a set of goals, and you have a set of goals of what you're going to do this week. You have a date night set every single week. You have some specific things that you put in place to allow you to find value that brings excitement to the relationship.

Create a bucket list for your relationship with things you want to do as a couple. Do this together. So when you have all these things that you're working towards, that's what I would call a fulfilled relationship. You're always working towards something exciting, just to have fun with your relationship.

Create a fantasy jar. Sit down with your spouse and talk about your fantasies, both for your sexual fantasies and your relationship fantasies. Stick with only the things with your spouse. All fantasies have to be monogamous. You may have a fantasy of having sex in a dressing room with your spouse. Who knows? You may have a fantasy of doing it in the car. Who knows? But you're looking for things that you can talk about together and share in what we call the no-judgment zone.

You look at your spouse and say, "Look. There's no judgment here at all. I want to hear your fantasies." More importantly, you're going to take all these fantasies and you're going to write them down. You're going to put them on a piece of paper. You're going to fold it up to where you can't see what it is, and you're going to drop it in a jar. You may get 10 of them. You may get 20 of them. You're each going to put fantasies in the jar. Then one day a week, one day a month, you're going to prioritize a day and pull a fantasy out of the jar to fulfill that day. That's crazy, isn't it? But imagine the excitement, because you don't know what the fantasy's going to be that day. You may have something that you're like, "Oh my. I never saw that coming."

It's about creating excitement and keeping excitement in your relationship. Create a fantasy jar. Keep things spontaneous. Keep them adventurous. You can just walk in the door one day from work and say, "Hey, honey, let's pull something out of the fantasy jar." Then, boom, you pull something out, and you're having the wildest night ever. She could have a fantasy where you to dress up like Superman. You could have a fantasy where you want her to dress up like Wonder Woman. Just enjoy your relationship with your spouse. Create things that give it value. Create things that keep excitement in your relationship. Your wife's going to be so in love with you. Your husband's going to be so in love with you and so excited all the time that they have something to look forward to. They can't wait for fantasy night. You can create what you call fantasy night once a month, once a week, or whatever it is. Imagine the excitement that you're each going to feel because you have no idea what's going to come out of that jar.

How exciting is that? Your relationship is going to be like, "Oh, my god." You're not going to know what hit you. Have fun with your relationship. You and your spouse deserve greatness, love, value, validation, compassion, kindness, truth and honesty. Give of yourself to your spouse. Stop looking for ways to be negative and look for ways to create life in the relationship. When you're creating life, you're preventing the affair from happening, because they're not going to want to go talk to someone about how bad the relationship is, they're going to go talk to people like how amazing the relationship is. It's up to you. You get a choice.

"Our Marriage will be great when we decide to make it great."
~ Eric F. Rios

If you find yourself in need of 1 on 1 marriage coaching, couples marriage coaching, or an intensive workshop, (Marriage by Design Workshop), contact us via website: **www.thesmilingmarriage.com**.

Chapter 8

Kids & Step Kids

I have to tell you this is a really exciting subject for me because I've been a parent for almost 25 years now. I can tell you by raising both boys and girls what an adventure it is. Raising kids is full of ups and downs, and it's different with each child. Yes, it can be hard at times. Sometimes you think to yourself, does it ever get better? Is it ever going to end? Am I losing my mind? There are things you think to yourself that you would have never expected you'd think about raising kids.

We've all seen a few parents that seem to have easy kids. They didn't have any problems or issues. It was really just a great time raising that child. Of course, their second child might be bouncing off the walls. You just didn't know what you're going to get with him or her. That was a child that you were just losing your mind over and your hair is turning gray.

A friend of mine said that if his fourth kid would have been his first kid, they wouldn't have kids ever again. We would have stopped right there. That goes to show you that kids can be an adventure. You just don't know what you're going to get. You could get a good kid, a bad kid, a tall kid, a skinny kid. You might click with your child or you may have a personality conflict. I'm telling you it's just crazy.

I used to always joke around years ago and I would tell people, "I got a great business. It's called rent-a-kid." This is for people who want to have kids. I'm going to rent you a kid who likes to get in trouble or a kid who's got a smart mouth. Would you like to see if you really want kids? It was a fun joke because people didn't realize that having kids can be such an adventure, and it can be so crazy in so many ways because you've never done this before. You finally entered the state of parenthood but you didn't get a manual.

You just don't know what's going to work, because what works for one child may not work for the other. I can tell you what works for all, and that's patience. We all wish we had a guide that said, "This is what you do when your kid comes home and has a bad grade, gets in trouble at school, or even gets suspended. This is what you're supposed to do to make the biggest impact on your child to make sure they make better choices the next time."

However, I think a guide would take all the fun out of being a parent. One of the funniest parts about being a parent, is not knowing what's going to happen next. We all have great stories we can share when it comes to being a parent. You don't know where it's going to go, what your child is going to do. You don't know what's going to happen.

I can tell you when my middle son was around 2 or 3 years old, I remember him going out of a window onto the roof of our apartment. How he figured out how to do this, I have no idea. I stepped outside to talk to the neighbor and then I look up and there he is standing on the roof of the house and I'm screaming, "Caleb, get your butt back in that window." He ran and he dove through that window. Who would have ever thought that a boy that age could open a window, pop the screen and get out on the roof? Who in their right mind thinks their kids are going to do something like this? Nobody. We just don't always know what we're going to get when we have kids.

I used to climb trees when I was really young and jump off roofs of houses. I just had no filter of making intelligent decisions when I was a child. Most girls tend to talk. They do a lot of play. They do a lot of communication. Boys? They're making noise all the time. They're making noise, destroying things, testing the tensile strength of things.

I have a grandson who is 23 months old, and I've watched him test the tensile strength of everything he picks up. He picks it up and bends it as far as he can to see if it snaps. If it snaps, he grabs something else. We'll outside in the yard and he'll pick up a stick, and what's the first thing he does? He tries to bend it. You give him a toy, what's the first thing he does? He'll see how strong it really is.

Every kid is different. Every kid is unique in their own way. Sometimes we as parents need to learn to be patient with our kids and understand that it's going to be okay. It's probably going to turn out well.

Mean What You Say

The most important thing I'll ever tell you is this is say what you mean and mean what you say. If you're not going to do it don't tell them. If you're not going to do something don't tell them.

I here parents tell their kids all the time, "I'm not telling you again. I'm not telling you again," and then you'll hear the same thing five minutes later. Kids are intelligent. They've already figured this out. They've already figured out how many times you're going to tell them not to do something before you really get serious.

A simple way of making that stress, that headache and that heartache go away is mean what you say, say what you mean, or don't say it. Don't raise your kids to know and believe that what you say really doesn't matter, because that's what they're going to think of you. They're going to think less of you.

Let me tell you something. Growing up I wasn't the best kid at all. I was given all the freedom in the world to make stupid choices. I did what I wanted to do when I wanted to do it, and how I wanted to. When I became a parent, I knew I wanted my kids to be good kids. I wanted them to behave. I wanted them to be the kind of kid that was respectful. I knew in order to do that I really needed to focus on teaching them respect and making sure they understood what respect was, and setting higher expectations for them. Not unrealistic expectations, but behavioral expectations as far as what I expected out of them.

When you look at raising your own kids, you have a mother and a father together. You're doing this together as a team. The one thing my wife hated was how when I walked in the door, all of a sudden the kids shaped up. They knew that my expectations were X and hers were Y. They knew without a doubt that when dad walked in the door, dad was serious. Dad expected you to do these things. They didn't take her as seriously as they took me. They look at her as someone they could get over on, so it took a lot of support from me to make sure I supported her, to make sure the kids understood, "Look, you have to respect her the same way you respect me." Let me tell you this isn't always easy, but it's so worth it.

Parental Involvement

I read a study years ago that looked at whether kids were more successful in life if they went to a public school or private school. The study found that the school choice didn't affect the student's success in life, but parental involvement did. Ask yourself this, are we the kind of parents that don't really give our kids attention, don't give them time because we have to do that, it's very important?

When you're raising your kids together, as a couple, as a team, it makes it so much easier because your kids have support from both sides. They've got a great balance, but most importantly let your kids be kids. Allow them to be kids. Allow them to make mistakes. Allow them to make bad choices within a set of boundaries you've given them. You've got to look at what your boundaries are first of all, and then you can tell your children, "As long as you stay within these boundaries, we're going to be okay." Each one of your kids is going to be different as far as how you give them boundaries. Not every child gets the same boundaries because kids are different.

When you're doing this together as a couple, as a mother and a father, it makes it so much easier because you're working together as a team to help that child succeed, not just in school but in their behaviors and their attitudes and their personalities. We're lifting them up. We're inspiring them. We're building their self-confidence. We're building their self-esteem. We're making our kids a priority as far as their images. We need to always be looking at ways to build our kid's self-image.

I went on a mission trip to the country of Panama and I remember to this day what the minister said. He asked if it was really that big of a deal if your child didn't get a perfect grade. Is it really such a big deal, and worth destroying our kid's self-esteem and self-worth? Do they have to fit into a certain mold? I know we do this with the positive intent. We want them to be well, but I realized that day that I had to stop being so hard and allow them to be kids and allow them to flourish into something great.

I came home from that mission trip changed as a parent because I realized what I was doing was doing more harm than it was doing well. I didn't allow my kids to be kids, show them I trusted them, allow them to make choices, and allow them to fail.

Just to allow your kids some space and some freedom and don't take things so seriously. Realize that your kids are going to probably turn out great. When you look back on your life, you're going to say, "I was pretty hard on them, but it was for their own good." No, it's not always for their own good. It's for your good. We're hard so often because it benefits us as parents, because it gives us the peace of mind, and makes us look good, and because we do not want to trust them.

Teach your child natural consequences. Tell them, "If you stay within these boundaries I'm going to give you some freedom. If you fall out of these boundaries, I have to tell you there's going to be a consequence." This is the way life works. If you don't listen and do the things that we have asked to stay within these boundaries there are going to be consequences and you may not like them. I may have to take some of your freedoms away until you can show us we can trust you again.

Remember parents, remember this. You're going to get through this. Your kids are going to get through this. This is going to pass. Work together as a team, as a couple and bring togetherness to the family. Bring togetherness through the relationship with your children.

The most important thing you can do with your kids in this position is be there for them every day. If you're the parent who didn't get custody but you only get the one day a week, go to every single event that they have. Go be at the practice. Sit there and watch them. Be a part of your kid's life. If they have a game, make sure you go to the game. Make your kids a priority. Your kids are dying for that attention. They're dying for you to be there and be a part of their lives. They want you to be there.

Many parents miss this. They feel like, "I don't see my kids anyway, so what's the big deal." The big deal is that it's a big deal to them. It's a big deal to your kids. Your kids will go through their entire life wishing that their parents were there in their life. Your kids are going to go through their entire life and say, "Man, I wish I could have gotten to know my mom or dad better."

Kids want you to look them in the eye and tell them, "I'm so proud of you." Instead we tend to focus more on all the negative things that our kids do. We tend to focus on the bad grade that they get. We tend to focus on the little problems that they come up with, their little cries for attention. If we could just learn to be intentional about giving them value, building their self-esteem and building their self-worth, not looking at them and tell them they're stupid, not looking at them and telling them that they're the worst kid in the world.

Don't tear your kids down. Raise your kids up to have a positive self-esteem, to have confidence in themselves. Look at your kids every day and tell them, "You are amazing. I'm so proud of you. I love you." When you look at your child and you tell them you love them, it's going to do wonders for them. You don't even realize how powerful this is.

The crazy part is you spent the first 10 years of your kid's life telling them these things, and then you might have stopped. What happened? They became a teenager and they started being a normal kid influenced by others. All of a sudden we're focused on all the bad. We're focused on all the things they're not doing right. Their teacher sends a note home from school and says, "Your kid is not doing very well." Instead of looking at all the positive that they've done and try to build up their strengths, we focus on that one little negative thing.

I always felt the purpose of grounding was to make sure we stayed out of the parents' way. That was my opinion as a kid. Your kids deserve the very best they can get. Your kids deserve to see you building them up on a daily basis. Your kids deserve this. Remember this: you wanted those children in most cases. That child didn't have to be born into your home. You chose to have that child born into your home. It is up to you to build that child's self-esteem. It is up to you to raise them up to be something great.

Don't tear them down. Don't tell them bad things. Don't tell them it's their fault. Give them some value. Your kids deserve that because one day they're going to be an adult and they're going to model what they see in you. Your kids need love and they need love every day. They need it, not just through your words but they need it through your actions. They need to see it in you every single day. They need to see it in the relationship that you have.

Protect your kids. Protect their hearts. Protect their minds. Pour into your kids. Pour love and compassion and kindness into your kids. Give them the value that they deserve. Don't take it so serious. Allow them to be kids. Allow them to make good choices. Allow them to make bad choices. Find a punishment that works for you with your kids.

I didn't want to be someone who held things over their head. I wanted them to know that they made a bad choice. We talked about it. They understand it, so now let's go have a great day. Let's focus on what we want to do versus staying focused on the little negative thing that happened. We don't hold grudges as parents. We don't want to teach our kids to hold grudges. Are you serious? Why in the world would you ever want to teach your kid to hold a grudge? You know how you teach them that? By modeling that to them.

The most important thing you can do for your child is to love that child, but love them through your actions not just through your words.

"His" Kids

The reason I want to talk about our kids, his kids, her kids, and step kids is because when you get into a relationship where you are going to become a stepparent, it can be a little more of a challenge for you. You take a group of kids that were in a home that was separated. It's torn apart for whatever reason. It's going to make things harder.

The father has his own ideas on how he wants to raise kids. He is doing what he thinks is best for them. It may not be what you think is best for them. Many fathers end up getting the kids maybe one day a week and every other weekend, or 2 days a week, every other weekend. Some guys they just split it down the middle 50/50, but they're his kids.

With his kids he's going to do what he thinks is best. There's always a positive intent in everything he does. He may be the kind of parent that lets him do whatever they want to do, because he only gets to see them 1 day a week and every other weekend, so he wants to make sure it's the best time ever. You'll say, "That's not the best thing for them," but to him it is. You may not agree with it, but to him there's positive intent there to make sure he builds and keeps that relationship with his kids because he only gets to see them once a week. He's not trying to be the parent who is overbearing. He's trying to be the parent who cares and wants to provide value for his kids. He's going to have his own way of raising his kids. He's going to have his own reasons for raising his kids in certain way.

We don't want to knock his process, his way of doing things. What we want to do is support him and help him, help him be the very best parent he can be. It's not by telling him, "You're doing the wrong job. You're doing a bad job. You're not doing it right." That doesn't bring any value to anybody, because remember to him he's doing what he knows. We always do what we know and that's it.

"Her" Kids

Many women get the kids on a regular basis, even much more than the male will in many cases. But there are also cases where the male will get the kids first. He'll raise the kids. She gets one day a week, every other weekend or they split it in some way. More and more parents are splitting time 50/50.

Remember when you're the parent who gets the kids more of the time, you get to put a more structured regimen in place because you've got them every day almost. That can also mean that you no longer have that support to help you accomplish things that you need to accomplish. Now you're doing the yard work, you're doing the other things, you're raising the kids, you're cooking dinner, and your life has become so challenging in so many ways.

The one with the kids tends to be really harsh about how the other parent parents the kid, because they want a strict regimen to be followed on a daily basis. When you're the one who doesn't have the kids, all of a sudden you have found all this freedom to do whatever you want to do.

This becomes an enormous challenge for many parents, because you have now been put in a position where you are a single parent raising your kids all by yourself and it hurts. It's tough. You feel this loneliness. You feel constant pressure to perform as a mother or father, as a worker, and as a provider. You feel that pressure because your kids were used to this lifestyle of getting whatever they wanted in many ways.

You went down to one income per household. You've got your mortgage payment. You've got your car payments. The kids have to give up because of what has happened. You feel this pressure as a parent and it hurts you. It tears you apart inside, because you want to be the very best to your kids that you could be. You want to provide the best opportunities ever. You want to provide the very best solution for your kids.

When we look at her kids, she's the one raising them all by herself. She's getting stricter with them. She has to be, because she's got a bigger challenge on her plate over the one who doesn't have the kids on a normal basis. Understand this. I know many men who have custody of their kids and they have the same challenge. We need to realize that each parent has their own parenting style and they have a reason for doing what they do, and all of the things that they do have a positive intent to it. There's always a positive outcome in what they want to do.

Step Kids

We're going to go into the very important topic of step kids. We've talked about our kids, his kids, her kids. Let's talk about step kids. I've been a stepparent for much of my adult life. I was raised in stepparent family. I hated my stepfather. I absolutely hated him. I felt he didn't like me. Maybe I was wrong, but I determined that through his actions towards me.

When you look at step kids, some people give them these labels. They always talk about, "You're the redheaded stepchild." The parents get labels like the wicked stepmother, the wicked stepfather. It doesn't make any sense. You need to understand that that child did not ask to be put in this situation.

You'll say, "They're not my kids. They're not my concern." No, they are going to become your concern. If you're going to intentionally get into a relationship where the other person has kids, you need to pay attention to what I'm going to tell you. We can't look at them as "her" or "his" kids. We need to go into this relationship understanding that these kids may be extremely angry at the circumstances at hand. They're very upset because their mom and their dad have separated. They may feel the guilt. They may carry this guilt every day like it's their fault.

There may be some anger involved, and the new kids may look at you as the problem. They might even think you stole their mom or dad from their other parent. Many times they're going to be so upset at the circumstances, and then we walk into this relationship with these kids. We expect those kids to listen to what we have to say. We expect them to respect us. We think, "I'm a parent. I'm an adult. You should adamantly respect me." We don't think about the fact that they're hurt so bad inside. They're devastated. Their lives have been turned upside down and all we can think about is ourselves. We forget to think about the kids, because our focus on is what we're going to get out of this relationship.

I saw a show about a couple where the stepfather told the stepdaughter that this house would be a perfect house if she didn't live there. Why wouldn't this child want to leave, want to run away, when there's no value being given in this home? Why would the mother allow that to happen? Our kids are so important. Our kids deserve the very best from us. Our kids deserve our patience, our kindness, our respect.

When you look at a stepchild, don't see them as "their" kids. See them as your very own kid or kids. See them as a child who is hurting deeply inside who needs to be loved and shown compassion. Allow them to be angry. Don't try to rule over them with an iron fist, trying to get them to comply to every order that you bark out. Set the standards. Set the boundaries as a couple. When you go into this relationship, go to the mother or the father, whoever the primary is and say, "Look, I'm going to support you here."

If my boys were ever disrespectful to my wife, I always chastised them because she was their stepmother. I made it a point to chastise them and make sure they understood, "Guys, you have to respect her." I also made it a point to her to make sure she understood not to take it personally.

Remember this: these kids didn't ask to be thrown into your drama. They didn't ask to be thrown into your world, into your world of heartache, into your world of pain. They didn't ask to be put into this lifestyle of hate and anger that they see going back and forth with the parents. They're so innocent in almost all cases when it comes to being shoved off into your home. Show some patience to your kids. Show some love to your kids. Don't let your step kids get the short end of the stick.

I understand that if you have your own kids and you're a stepparent that you're going to have a closer relationship to your own children. There's nothing wrong with that. I understand that both individuals are probably going to do this. They're going to lean more towards their own child at times. I get that, but don't forget that other child is watching you, that other child wants some love and wants some attention as well.

Remember that your parenting style isn't the only style that works. Remember every parent has their own parenting style. Come together with a collaborative style so you both can be good co-parents and make sure you're helping these children succeed, not tearing them apart and pushing them out of the home.

Don't be one who bashes the other parent. Don't be one who tears them apart. You're angry, your kids are angry, your kids are hurt, you're hurt and things come out of your mouth. If you do these things, give yourself some grace as well. If you do it in front of your kids, go to your kids and say, "Look, I'm sorry. I shouldn't say that. I'm sorry, and that wasn't the right thing to say this time."

If you get into an argument with your spouse in front of your kids, make up in front of your kids. Teach them both sides. Let them see both sides. It is okay to disagree. Model the behavior. Model the behavior with your actions as the way you want your kids to be. Show them the same mercy you want to be shown. Show them the same love that you're craving and desiring and wanting so badly. Give your kids that chance to thrive and become the very, very best kids they can become. Your kids deserve nothing less than that from you.

Set aside your own personal agenda when it comes to your kids. Your kids deserve the very best you that they can get. They deserve to be valued. Stop seeing them as step kids and start seeing them as children who deserve to be loved. Learn to change your own behavior if you expect your kids to change their behavior. Learn to provide value to your kids. It will be amazing at the response you get from your kids when you provide them value.

Being a parent is a challenge all by itself. Being a parent is the biggest, most challenging task you'll ever take on. You're going to have this challenge for about 18 years. It's going to take you about 18 years to go through this. You're going to make good choices as a parent. You're going to make bad choices as a parent, but I can assure you of one thing. You will get through this.

If you could put patience and love and kindness on your side and make that the priority of your life, I can assure you it will be a very different life when you get to the end. I can assure you that your kids are going to see things from a very different perspective. They're going to see through eyes of love and eyes of compassion. Kids just want to be loved. They want to be valued. They want to be built up, and they want to be held up to the world as somebody great in your eyes.

Kids love to hear these words: I'm proud of you; I love you; you're amazing; you're very special; I love being your parent; I'm always here for you; whatever you need just let me know. Kids love to be lifted up and valued.

We talked about our kids, his kids, her kids and step kids and most important we talked about kids. Kids need value. Give them the value they need and watch their lives change. Build them up, build them up, and build them up. Don't take things personally. They're just kids. They're learning. Just like you as a parent, they're learning. Allow them to be kids. Set your boundaries and give them value.

"No great marriage was ever built on good intentions."
~ Eric F. Rios

If you find yourself in need of 1 on 1 marriage coaching, couples marriage coaching, or an intensive workshop, (Marriage by Design Workshop), contact us via website: **www.thesmilingmarriage.com**.

Chapter 9

52 Weeks of Love

I'd like to thank my wife, Shelly Rios, for helping with this bonus chapter which shares 52 weeks of love, an idea for every week of the year. When you are constantly being intentional in creating love in your marriage you find yourself in a much better place with your spouse. Take the time to go through this chapter and find something that you can do each week to keep love alive in your relationship. Have fun with your relationship and keep the love alive!

1. Buy flowers. This doesn't have to be a special occasion. In fact, the ones I love the most are when it's just for no reason at all. Buy your spouse some flowers, bring them home, take them to their work, whatever it may be, just do it.

2. Bake something together. If you don't like to do it, your spouse will find it even more exciting because she knows you didn't like to do it the first place. There's a little sacrifice involved when you bake something for your spouse.

3. Have breakfast in bed. Come downstairs early in the morning, make breakfast, and bring it to your spouse as a surprise.

4. Bring your partner a sweet dessert. You just stop by the bakery, you grab her favorite dessert or his favorite dessert, and you just bring that to them, and you surprise them with it. Maybe you could even take them upstairs into the bedroom and surprise them with it. You get to make this fun.

5. Cook dinner together. Maybe make it fun and do it naked. Obviously, hopefully your kids are not around, but cook dinner together in the kitchen while not dressed or maybe you have your apron on and nothing else underneath it. Just be funny, be fun, and cook dinner naked.

6. Create a vision board of goals and dreams. Write down your most fascinating life, take pictures of the car you would love to have the most, of the house you would love to have the most, the vacation. Create a vision board and have a fun time creating that vision board and just dream together as a couple.

7. Dance in the kitchen. This could be anytime during the day, whether you're cooking or not. Just crank up the music and start dancing with your spouse. The best part of it, is your kids will probably be laughing at you and taking pictures but who cares, do it anyway. Dance in the kitchen.

8. Do a treasure hunt with clues. Now, doing a treasure hunt can be a lot of fun. You can go to work in the morning, leave your spouse a list of things to find, but it's a treasure hunt so they're going to find the first one. Then they'll get the next clue. Maybe they end up at lunch with you at the end. Just make a treasure hunt and make it a lot of fun while you do it.

9. Dress up and meet your spouse at the door. Now this could be for anything. This could be, you know, your spouse had a bad day and you're home first, and you're going to dress up and welcome them home with open arms. In some cases maybe you want to dress down as the spouse comes home from work. You decide how you want to be, and how creative you want to be. Just do it for them when they get home.

10. Dress your spouse. This could be fun. This could be for work or if you're going out, but help your spouse get dressed. Help pick out their clothes. Say, "Hey, I really like that shirt. Why don't you put that on?"

11. Exercise together. Exercising together is huge. You're going to work out together, you're going to get healthy together, and you're on the same page working towards the same outcome and the same goal.

12. Have a fire place date. Have you ever just sat down in front of a fire place? It's cold outside, the snow is on the ground, it's just so beautiful, and you just sit there with your spouse, get the fire going and bring a glass of wine. You bring the dinner over there and you just setup a little date in front of your own fireplace.

13. Flirt with each other. There are so many spouses out there that forget about flirting. It doesn't have to be that way.

Flirt with your spouse anytime day or night. My husband and I constantly walk by each other and just tickle each other, or he likes to playfully swat me on the rear. Either way, flirt with your spouse whether be in your home, outside of the home, in the car, just make it sparky, and make it fun. Just don't forget to do it.

14. Go bicycling. It's a great time to have time together. You get to go outside and get some great exercise. You get to see some great scenery. If you have bad knees, it's really easy on the knees and body. Most importantly, it's time spent together. It's time that you prioritize spending time together. Maybe you go bicycle around the lake, around the pound, you go down the pretty trail. Bicycling is not just good for your health, it's good for your mind, and it's good for your togetherness.

15. Go have a picnic. Include it with bike riding or not, but go have a picnic, spend time together enjoying the scenery in front of a pond or at a park. Go people watch and talk about what you see, but the best thing is being together. It's just a quiet time with you and your spouse to go have a picnic and enjoy yourselves.

16. Go hiking. It doesn't have to be anything exorbitant or extravagant. It can be something that is small, but just go for a hike. Make hiking a priority because for once again it's good for your health, it's good for your mind, and it's good for you guys being together. You're doing something together. When you go hiking, there's no telling what you might see. Hiking also allows you to walk together and talk.

17. Go out to dinner together at a new restaurant. Try something you've never had before. A lot of times we're doing the same thing at the same place which is fine, but this time try something new. Be a little adventurous. Try new places and new foods.

18. Go to church together. Maybe try going to church or trying a new church. Just go to church together and make it a fun event where you get to go experiment and experience other people's lives. Great connection time.

19. Hold hands while driving. This is something that Eric and I try to do all the time. It's just awesome. Especially when you're driving in a car with an older couple and you see them holding hands and you just think that is so cute. One thing we're doing is we're modeling to our kids as well when they're sitting behind us they see us holding hands. They see that we care about each other even when we're in a car driving somewhere.

20. Listen to music together. Listen to your favorite tracks or the radio, or even share some ear buds. Find your favorite songs, those songs that bring you the passion and bring the passion back to the relationship. Do you have a copy of your wedding song? Just find those songs that bring back really positive memories in the relationship. The magic will happen again.

21. Go through your wedding album together. I love pictures and I have pictures all over the house and albums galore. Sit down and go through your actual wedding album together, remember those positive memories and take yourself back to that moment when times were exciting, and awesome, and you were looking forward to the rest of your life together. Bring back the positive memories and you will also bring back that spark.

22. Make a coupon booklet for redemption. What does that look like? Make a book with coupons for dinner, a back rub, grocery shopping or running errands, and even a date. Think of ways you can do things for your spouse and add value to their life. Make it a fun thing too, just make out some just wild off the wall things that you'll do. Be creative with it. Think of what you would love to do but also think about what your spouse would love to have done. Make a coupon booklet and make it fun, make it exciting, and make sure you redeem the coupons!

23. Open the door for your spouse every day for a week. Now this just doesn't have to be the man doing it for the woman, make it fun. People will probably laugh at you, especially if they do see a woman open the door for their spouse, their husband. Who cares what people think anyway? You're having fun. You're being goofy. Chivalry still exists, and it can exist on both sides, so open the car door for your spouse every day for a week and see what that does.

24. Plan a getaway vacation. Now this doesn't mean it has to be 7 days, 8 days, 10 days, or 2 weeks. It can just be just a simple 3 day little vacation. We leave on Friday, we come back on Sunday, but plan a getaway and make it a surprise. Make it a fun surprise for your spouse. If you have kids, make sure you've already planned a babysitter, you've already taken care of all the things you need to take care of to make this an exciting event.

During the getaway it's the time you rejuvenate. Your relationship comes back together. It creates closeness, it creates togetherness, and it creates that time when you're going to enjoy each other once again because it's just you two having a great time together.

25. Plan a spa day or golf outing or whatever your spouse enjoys. Time together is very important, but sometimes it's also fun to do something on your own as well, especially if your spouse plans it for you. Maybe plan a day for each of you and then meet up afterwards. The husband can go play golf while the wife gets a massage or her nails done, and then you can have dinner. That will be so exciting to get time on your own and then you meet back together feeling rejuvenated, fresh and excited.

26. Pray together. Praying together is just spending some time of devotion together, time of maybe meditation for you, or just praying. It's just a time of being quiet together and just meditating on the same thing and praying for the same things. You're working together for a similar outcome or peace in the family, or some peace in your relationship.

It can be anything, but just spend some time praying together. Hold hands while you pray. Bring togetherness, hug while you pray, and kiss while you pray. Just pray together. Make praying a fun thing and have a great time with it.

27. Recreate your first date. Go to that same restaurant, sit at that same table, or go to that same play, or whatever your first date may have been. Ours was a little Mexican restaurant, and we still remember exactly that day and which table we sat at. Sometimes we sit there and remember that fun night of our first date and bring those positive memories back.

28. Renew your vows privately. It's one thing to renew your vows openly to the public and for others to see. In some manner that's just a big show for everybody else to see and it's not really for you. When you renew your vows privately, and it's just you and your wife, and you look at each other in the eye, and you begin to recite the vows that you said the day you got married.

Or you may have recreated some new vows for your life, but just renew your vows privately. It's amazing what could happen. It's amazing the emotions it's going to pull out of you. It's amazing how you're going to feel alive and you're going to feel so loved, and you're going to feel like, "Oh my God he or she loves me so much," because you've taken the time to renew and recommit to your vows that you made all those years ago.

29. Run outside and kiss in the rain. One thing we love in our family is when it rains and there are storms. We immediately go outside and check out the sky and watch the storm come in. This time run in the rain and go kiss, or just play in the rain like a big kid. We have kids ranging from many ages, so we have plenty of time to be kids ourselves and enjoy the time with our kids. Run and play in the rain. The kids enjoy doing it with us as well.

30. Have a scavenger hunt. Just create it between you and your spouse but this is a little different kind of scavenger hunt. This isn't just your average scavenger hunt. It has a happy ending. You're going to do something off the wall crazy for the one who wins that scavenger hunt between you and your spouse. You could make the scavenger hunt in your house, you can make it down the street, you can make it in the street, and you can make it wherever you want to make it. Remember, the scavenger hunt comes with something very special, and that's a happy ending for the winner.

31. Send your spouse a loving or flirty text message. Just out of the blue send them a text message saying, "Hey, love you," or "I'm thinking about you," or "I can't wait to see you," anything, even a, "Hi." Just send a simple text message. It goes a long way.

32. Share your dreams with your spouse. I believe many spouses are scared to death to share their dreams with their spouse. They're scared to share what they really want. They're scared to open up and talk about it. Now when your spouse is sharing their dreams, don't be judgmental, don't question them. Just learn to listen to their dreams and don't crush their dreams, don't tell them they can't have their dreams. Let them have a dream. Just listen to those dreams because you want those dreams to become a reality in your own life and share your dreams with each other. If you don't have a dream, find a dream because dreams are an amazing thing to work towards. Just find something that you can talk about.

See what this is doing for you. By sharing your dreams, it's opened up the line of communication between the both of you. You're not talking about the everyday problems that you have or your kids, this is talking about you, you, you, and you. Make it about your partner when they're sharing their dreams, open your heart and listen. Once you both have shared your dreams, look for ways to help you each find a way to have those dreams fulfilled.

33. Stargaze together. We enjoy watching the stars from anywhere. One of my favorite spots is lying on our trampoline. It's so comfortable. If you've never tried it, it's just like a water bed but you're outside and enjoying the stars and the sky and the moon. One of our favorite things to do as long as it's not raining is to lie on our trampoline and just watch the stars and hope to see a shooting star.

34. Take a bubble bath together. Turn the lights down, put a candle on, put some music on, and put some aroma in the air. You know that typically leads to a happy ending. Come on now, let's be serious here, let's be adults. Take a bubble bath together and have fun. During your bubble bath, maybe share your dreams; share your times that you love together. Talk, open up, communicate, because everything you do here is about communication, it's about bringing togetherness, coming closer.

35. Take a dance class together. Now to some, this is probably something that you would not be interested in doing but others are. In fact, our wedding dance was a surprise to all of our family and friends. We didn't take an actual class together at a community center, instead we bought a DVD and we actually taught ourselves the Cha Cha. During our first dance at our wedding reception, we started off with their normal slow song that we both picked, and then about a minute and a half into the dance, the DJ switched the song to a Latino song and we kicked it up and started doing the Cha Cha. Everybody laughed and cheered and mostly laughing at us, but either way it was a lot of fun. It was a surprise to everyone and we just had a blast doing it. Take a dance class together or learn how to do a dance on your own. It's fun.

36. Take a night swim together. If you don't have a pool, get a hotel room with one. Go take a night swim even if you go to a lake, beach or river. Just go take a night swim and have some fun with it. That can be a lot of fun time together.

37. Take a road trip. Now this doesn't have to be hours and hours away, it could just be a short trip up the highway or check out some scenery. We often do this in the winter when we're going eagle watching. Around our area we drive up to the rivers and it's so beautiful to see the eagles flying over you. Take a road trip together, just you and your spouse, grab your favorite candy and snack. Ours is peanut M&Ms and licorice. We stop at the store, we get our candy, and we just hit the road. Sometimes not having an ending, we just drive wherever it takes us. That makes it fun and adventurous and it helps keep that spark alive in your marriage. Take a road trip together.

38. Take a walk. Walking is one of the healthiest things you could do for your heart. It is such a healthy thing you guys can do together. The further you walk, the more you get to talk. The longer you go, the longer you're together. If you walk a mile, it's going to take you around 15 minutes. If you walk two miles, you're looking at it about half an hour. Three miles, 45 minutes and that can be such great time to rejuvenate and create great conversation while you're out taking a walk.

Walking is great for your heart health, it's great for your body, and it's great for your mind. It is a great way to just reconnect each day. If you could take a walk once a week or every single day, whatever it is just make sure taking a walk is in your to-do-list as a couple. While you're walking, make sure you talk.

39. Tell each other 3 things that you appreciate about them. Again open the lines of communication. Just sit down one day and say, "Honey, I want to tell you these 3 things or more I appreciate about you and what I love about you or what I love when you do." Just 3 things to say, "Hey, you mean a lot to me. I appreciate you." Just make it personal and just do it.

40. Tell them you like them. In most relationships, you'll find that a spouse will say I love you a lot. "I like you" is less common. That's a huge thing. You got to like him because you can love him and hate him at the same time. If you hate him, you're probably not going to like him. Just look at him or her and say, "I like you. I really like being around you."

"I like the relationship we have. I like what we do together. I like our life together, but most importantly I like you. You bring me peace and you bring me happiness." Tell them you like them.

41. Undress your spouse. This could turn to something really fun or it could just be a quick little goofy thing.

Oftentimes, I come home from work and I want to get comfortable. I have my work clothes on with heels and pantyhose, and I want to just get in sweats or shorts or whatever it may be. I'll wink at my husband and say, "Hey, honey. Can you come help me get undressed?"

Sometimes that means I'm initiating something else, especially if kids aren't around. He'll come upstairs and help me get undressed. Do it when they get home from work, right before bed, and make it fun.

42. Volunteer together. Volunteer for something there where you can both give value back to the community. While you are giving value back to the community, you're feeling that value within yourself. You're feeling fulfilled that you've given value but you've done it together as a couple. This is about you creating the connection and keeping the connection going throughout your entire marriage.

As long as you're consciously focusing on commitment and connection, you're going to have connection and commitment. You're going to have a great life, you're going to have a great marriage, but you have to focus on this, that's why we're telling you to volunteer together and make this a lot of fun. Make a difference in somebody else's life.

43. Wash the car together and do it in a bathing suit. This can turn into a huge water fight, but go out there wash the car, have good intentions, and then just let the water flow. Shoot your spouse with water hose; drench them with a bucket of soap, whatever you want to do. Just make sure you close the car doors first! Again it's something fun and goofy, something that still needs to be done.

44. Watch the sunrise or sunset together. Have you ever sat on a beach, looked out at the sky, heard the waves, and watched as the sun begins to set. It gets a little bit lower and the beauty of it is just an amazing feeling. You begin to sit closer to your spouse, you begin to cuddle up together and you just stare into the sun, and you just stare into the sky watching the sunset. It brings you so close, and you don't have to say a word, but yet you just sat there in the sun, watching the sunset. Or you wake up early in the morning so you can see the sunrise; you see the beauty what the sun looks like when it rises. Now all of a sudden you're closer together and you start your day out close with togetherness.

45. Write down 25 things you love about your spouse. Again keeping the lines of communication open. List them out, send them to your spouse in an e-mail or sit down and talk about them. Share that list with them. I mean sometimes maybe it's embarrassing or maybe you'd rather them read it and then talk about it. Whatever you're comfortable doing, but just write 25 things down that you love about your spouse and share that with them.

If they're having a bad day, guess what that's going to do. That's going to make them smile, and they're going to get in a good mood really fast. Help them and help yourself. Write down 25 things that you love about your spouse.

46. Buy a gift. I have a friend of mine who likes to buy his wife a gift every single week. He said "I've done this for 20 years; I bought her a gift every single week." Can you imagine how much she loves getting those gifts? Can you imagine how she feels? She's always excited about getting something special from her husband, something different every single week.

It could be just a carnation, it could be a piece of candy, and it could be a pencil. Who knows what it could be. It can be anything you wanted it to be, but it's about giving value to your spouse and buying them a gift every single week, or just buying them a gift one time. Just make sure you take the time to bring value to relationship and buy them a gift. It doesn't have to be anything extravagant but just make it fun.

47. Give your spouse a massage. Who does not love massages? It can be shoulders, it can be feet, and it can be back. If you're having a bad day, sometimes I'm tense, I sit at the computer all day and I just need my shoulders rubbed a little bit. It's awesome when I say, "Honey, can you massage my shoulders?" Then he does it. Just give your spouse a massage. It shows that you care about them that you want them to feel good when they're not. Then again, it's touching, it's togetherness. Everything is a bonus. Give your spouse a massage.

48. Leave love notes. This could be on the bathroom mirror, this could be in your husband's lunch, in your wife's lunch, this could be on the dash of their car, and it could be on the window of their car. Love notes are exciting because there's something that you can do that's going to bring a little bit of excitement.

It's something that was unexpected. You didn't expect a note that says, "You look smoking hot today when you left for work." You don't expect that letter that says, "Hey, I just want you to know I thought you look really handsome today." Just leave love notes and make them fun, be creative with them, be crazy with them, be off the wall with them. You don't have to be normal when you leave a love note, make them just off the wall crazy something that says, "I can't wait for you to get home because ..."

49. Make your spouse's favorite dinner. Again, this can be combined with number 5 where you cook dinner together or you can do this on your own. Pick out their favorite meal, maybe again they're having a bad day or just a challenging week and they just want to feel good. Make them their favorite meal and surprise them. Something that they enjoy and it will put a smile on their face, so make them their favorite meal.

50. Take a bath together. Now, we talk about taking a bubble bath together. This can be just the same kind of thing, just make the time to create togetherness, come together as a couple. Come together that you're going to take a bath together, you're going to go to bed together. All these things are about bringing yourselves together as a couple. Just do the thing that brings joy to the relationship. Let's go take a bath together and have some fun with it.

51. Take your spouse a surprise lunch. Don't tell him you're coming. Obviously some work places are a little challenging to get into like mine, but tell them, "Hey, I'm bringing him lunch." Even if the person can't go to lunch or eat with you, still drop it off. Take them a surprise lunch. It will just make their day, it will make them smile and guess what, and it will make them think about you the rest of the day. Bring your spouse lunch.

52. Meet at home for little 'nooner' or quickie or some kind of fun. Relationships are about excitement. They're about love, they're about connection. Just maybe you guys say, "Hey, I'll meet you at the house. I'll see you there at 11:00, or I'll see you there at noon." That's where the word 'nooner' came from, you get it, right. Just be spontaneous.

You've already got the scene set for when they walk in the door, and they'll think, "Oh my, I never saw this coming. I love this. This is amazing." Meet at home for just something that's fun, not just lunch, but maybe just a little more than lunch. It comes with a really happy ending and watch what happens, when you go back to work you're smiling, you're excited.

We want you to take one item a week, or you can take more than one item a week, but make that a priority in your lives.

Now that you are at the end of this book you are left with some choices to make. The choice is always ours when it comes to having a good relationship. Make it a priority to give your relationship value and intention. When you give your relationship the intention that it needs, it begins to flourish. Be intentional about your behaviors and you'll watch your relationship grow in ways you never imagined. Be intentional about what you do every single day and be consciously aware of how your relationship is working, what you're doing, what's not working, and make it fun. Be spontaneous, be courageous, and be excited. Add to the list, create your own ideas, and do something each and every week to create that spark and keep you both smiling. I know that the Secret to Marriage has been revealed many times over and I hope by now you are applying this secret to your life now.

If you find yourself in need of 1 on 1 marriage coaching, couples marriage coaching, or an intensive workshop, (Marriage by Design Workshop), contact us via our website:

www.thesmilingmarriage.com

AUTHOR   SPEAKER   COACH

Check out our website for some exciting information and programs.

www.thesmilingmarriage.com

Private 1 on 1 Marriage Coaching with Eric Rios

Phone or Video Sessions

For more information on fees and schedule visit http://www.thesmilingmarriage.com/#!book-online/vhswy

15 min Power Coaching Session
30 Min Marriage Rehab Session
55 Min Marriage Rehab Session
And more

Marriage by Design Home Study Course

9 CD Audio Program

Marriage by Design Workbook

For more information or ordering visit our SHOP page at http://www.thesmilingmarriage.com

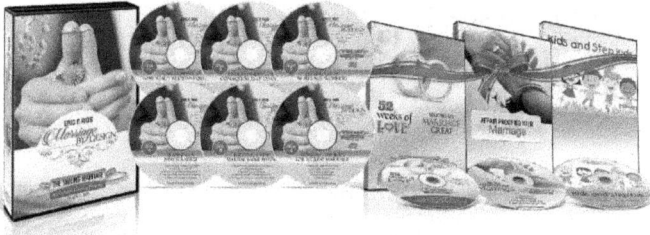

Speaking Services by Eric Rios

Eric Rios is a great speaker for:
- Special Events
- Keynote Speeches
- Conferences
- Executive Education
- Retreats
- Non-Profit Programs
- Professional Meetings

Available speaking formats:
- 30 Minute Keynote
- 60 Minute Keynote
- ½ Day Seminar
- Full Day Seminar
- Custom Workshops

For more information visit our page at
http://www.thesmilingmarriage.com

www.ingramcontent.com/pod-product-compliance
Lightning Source LLC
LaVergne TN
LVHW011418080426
835512LV00005B/123